"This book sounds the  arts education but au search in brain studie educational practices.

seasoned practice teaching and inspiring students."

Esther Lightcap Meek, PhD, Professor of Philosophy at Geneva College, Author of *Contact with Reality: Michael Polanyi's Realism and Why It Matters* and other books

"If the evangelical church wants to take seriously the challenges of secularism and its advances against the church, there is a pressing need for a pointed discussion about the intellectual formation of the next generation. McIlhenny's work offers an informed, broad, and insightful introduction to this much needed conversation. McIlhenny provides a fresh look at an ancient line of thinking, distills with care the key blessings in a Reformed liberal arts education, and shows how this education provides the foundation for a life well lived."

Ben Merkle, DPhil, President of New St. Andrews College

"Ryan McIlhenny constructs a new argument for the value of liberal arts education, appropriating the contributions of neuroscience to an understanding of human beings and their development as persons. Crucial is the brain's orientation to collative structures that tend toward an integral horizon within which research and learning are to take place. At the same time he uses his own Reformed Christian emphasis on the 'heart' as the integral, God-ward concentration point of concrete human existence that helps to buttress the Christian understanding of the mystery of the human creature in God's world. The result is a fresh and up-to-date defense of a venerable Christian educational project."

Bob Sweetman, PhD, H. Evan Runner Chair in the History of Philosophy and Academic Dean, Institute for Christian Studies

REFORMING THE LIBERAL ARTS

REFORMING THE LIBERAL ARTS

By
Ryan C. McIlhenny

FALLS CITY PRESS
Beaver Falls, Pennsylvania
www.fallscitypress.com

REFORMING THE LIBERAL ARTS

© 2017 Falls City Press

Published by Falls City Press
2108 Seventh Avenue
Beaver Falls, PA 15010
www.fallscitypress.com

Printed in the United States of America

Cover Design by Rafetto Creative
www.rafettocreative.com

Author Contact
rmcilhenny75@gmail.com

Publisher's Cataloging-in-Publication Data

McIlhenny, Ryan C., 1975—
        p. cm.
    Includes bibliographical references.
    ISBN: (paper) 978-0-9864051-2-9

    1. Church and college. 2. Church and college—United States.
I. Title.
    LC383.M142 2017   2017953249

To the Emersonian Cohort—intelligent, critical, creative, courageous, radical, godly, principled, dangerous.
You know who you are.

To R. Patrick Reeves, Juliette De Soto, Paul Otto, and Arnold Sikkema—true academics.

Contents

Acknowledgments

This work began as a labor of love. Having been raised on Reformational Philosophy, I had the great opportunity in 2007 to apply and articulate its tenets as I helped create the first fully-accredited Reformed institution of higher learning on the west coast. This included offering what became a successful core course where I introduced students to an understanding of a reformed approach to the liberal arts. The task of establishing an institution, aligning its mission with a radically (radix = root) biblical ground motive, and articulating such a vision for incoming students was one of the most rewarding experiences of my teaching career. The Lord has now graciously allowed me to extend such a pedagogical vision to the wider world of international education.

An educator's work means very little without students and fellow academics. Many of my former students will be familiar with the contents presented in this book. They've shared with me how influential Reformational Philosophy has been in their educational experience as well as in their lives now as not only parents, friends, and neighbors, but also professional writers, teachers, counselors, theologians, pastors, artists, lawyers, and philosophers. This book has been dedicated to these mature and Godly students. I also want to thank a few of my colleagues. First, my friend and fellow (or former) college-architect R. Patrick Reeves, who read the earliest (and possibly the most incoherent) draft of the manuscript, patiently offering his critical eye and constructive criticism. Second, big thanks goes out to my new friend and colleague, Keith Martel, editor and co-founder of Falls City Press. Keith has been very encouraging throughout the entire process. I cannot speak highly enough of his work through FCP. Thanks also to the handful of pre-publication readers, especially those intellectuals whom I've held in high regard for quite some time now: Robert Sweetman, Esther Meek, and Benjamin Merkle.

Finally, I wish to acknowledge my dear wife and partner Becky. She and I have been through quite a bit in the months leading up to the completion of the manuscript. We have experienced the great love of God as shown through his people in this our most difficult time. The Lord has been our defender against those who have sought our lives. Along with family and friends who have offered prayers and material support, Becky and I (and our kids) want to acknowledge the congregation of the Los Angeles Reformed Presbyterian Church for their continual love for our family.

RECOVERING THE LOST SPIRIT OF LEARNING

Like many graduate students in the final stages of completing their PhD, I landed an adjunct job teaching a weekly three-hour course at a local junior college. The class regularly included a ten-minute break. On one such break, I spoke with an older student who had a successful tech business, drove a beautiful sports car, and lived in one of the most expensive places in southern California (if not the country as a whole). I asked him why, if he had such a great job, a fine mode of transportation, and a most-coveted place to live, he was taking classes—humanities classes, mind you—at the college.

"Yeah, I have a lot of stuff," he responded. "But there's something missing. I want to know more about the world—about myself. I don't really know who I am." He was taking the time to finish his degree in order to make sense of it all, to put himself on the path toward meaning. This remained with me for quite some time.

What struck me was that although there was a gap in his life, or in the way he understood reality, he presupposed that there was something more. Material possessions could not "tie it all together." Drawing on the discussion, I began to see that self-knowledge demands, paradoxically, moving outside of the self. Knowledge not only requires an examination of the external world but also a coherent perspective that moves the learner beyond the temporal to the ultimate. In *Beyond the University*, Wesleyan University President Michael Roth claims that "education develops the capacities for seeing possibilities and for relishing the world across borders we might otherwise not have dared to cross. Education must lead us beyond these borders if it is to be more than training for a role that has already been allocated to us by the powers that be."[1] I'm not arguing for some kind of escapism from the world. Rather, I want to add to Roth by saying that an education "beyond the borders" requires faithful attendance to the things within the borders.

Going beyond the borders is the intent of a liberal arts education. This should pique the interest of those coming from a Christian perspective. Humans are more than flesh and blood, more than temporal beings, but have been made for transcendence—for eternity. Liberal arts educators work to make a coherent life-picture for their students, employing a variety of methods to break apart (analyze) and then put together (synthesize) reality. Doing so is the *telos* of learning, the path toward meaning. What is more, as this study proposes, meaning—to whatever degree—moves us beyond borders and in the direction of greater spiritual enrichment. Albert Einstein (1879-1955) once stated that science looks to "comprehension, as *complete* as possible, of the connection between the sense experiences in their totality, and, on the other hand, the accomplishment of this aim *by use of a minimum of primary concepts and relations* (seeking, as far as possible, logical unity in the world picture)."[2] This drive toward comprehension is, he said, *the* "cosmic religious feeling."[3] Humanity's pursuit of higher-order coherence, to make sense of a "challenging, changing, [and] confusing world," is, for James Ashbrook and Carol Albright, a religious activity. The brain desires an integrated whole: "Our human brain—with its imaginative symbolizing predisposition—is constantly sifting the messy world of randomness for the 'tiniest hints of order.'"[4] It satisfies this by connecting to an identifiable center, resting on a self-sufficient foundation from which we order the world. This drive toward coherence, "our most basic life-orientation," is, Albright and Ashbrook continue, "the pivotal expression of meaning seeking"—a "faith built into the activity of our biology, our nervous system, our neurocognitive processes."[5]

This book contends that a liberal arts education offers the best means not only to reintegrate mind and the world, but also to connect deeply with self, others, and God. The University of Notre Dame's Mark Roche recounts a story in which he approached a group of high school students and asked what they considered to be the "big issues" of life. Roche noted that the students' discussions ended with questions related to God and the importance of the self in the world:

> When I asked the students what philosophical questions most engaged them, they named quite a few, but two sets of questions dominated. The first set circled around God. The second revealed an innate interest in the natural world and a fascination with the place of the individual within the almost unfathomable vastness of the universe.[6]

As we draw *together* the multiple questions raised in a liberal arts context, we concomitantly draw *out* our religious root, what it is that we believe holds the cosmos together. For the Christian, the Triune God is not only the creator but also the sustainer of reality; He is the centerpiece that brings coherence. The more complex questions we raise, and the answers we discover, open further questions that bring us closer to the author of creation.

My emphasis here is not that a liberal education will bring us to a place where we can grasp the metaphysical, but rather that such an education is already embedded in a process of spiritual becoming, where the learner's awareness of his or her standing in relation to the author of life intensifies. The central claim of this book is simple: *A diverse liberal arts education pursues meaning as a holistic and spiritual enterprise that ends in divine peace.* Let's focus a bit more on this claim.

Meaning as Holistic

Since the time of Pythagoras, thinkers have understood beauty, along with truth and goodness, as a matter of proportion or harmony. The equation $2+2=4$ is true because it is a perfect proportion of parts to the whole; it is just (good) and pleasing (beautiful) to us. Such a claim—an argument in actuality—sits comfortably at the center of our being. When I encourage students to consider the cogency of an argument—and all teachers use argument and dialogue—I'm really asking them to consider the proportion or balance of the parts (supporting statements) with the whole (the major claim). The balance relates not only to the form of the argument itself but also to whether the evidence is offered in a fair and proportional manner.

Anyone can make a persuasive argument, but it must be backed by evidence. What is more, the argument must have a positive aesthetic affect for the individual and should lead to the cultivation of human flourishing. The same goals should apply when evaluating a mathematical theorem, a painting, a song, or a film. We can even say that a perfectly executed play by an athlete on the field or the court is not only beautiful, but also true. The young poet John Keats maintained the inextricable oneness of beauty, truth, and goodness: "Beauty is truth, truth beauty—that is all."[7]

Holistic Meaning as Religious

The relational nature of things endemic to meaning—meaning that includes proportion and harmony—is also connected to what many would consider the religious or the spiritual. Whenever we find ourselves making sense of the whole (piecing the world together), whether learning how to swing a club, solve an engineering problem, or perfecting that musical piece we've been working on, we reach not only greater meaning, but also experience a real moment of transcendence. Said differently, a flash of enlightenment, the point at which we see how things fit together in a beautiful mosaic, is akin to a religious experience. That which is meaningful is religious, furthermore, since its meaning comes in relation to God the Creator.

If relationality is essential to meaning, then God is also an essential part of all that we consider meaningful. Rejecting the relationality inherent to meaning is to reject God's place in meaning. The great Jonathan Edwards (1703-1753) once wrote that beauty and goodness consist of "a very complicated harmony; and all the natural motions and tendencies and figures of bodies in the universe are done according to proportion, and therein is their beauty." The harmony that humans encounter in creation is, Edwards writes, "the shadow of excellency"—God's excellence.[8] And the more in-depth the "excellency"—that is, the greater the proportion and harmony—the "nearer" humans "come to their creator."[9] When we examine the world and piece together coherent patterns—patterns that emerge through instruction from others and from our own observations—we draw closer to God.

This may be a good place for me to say that the argument I'm offering is an imminent one. Meaningful moments of profound coherence come in the process of learning. The strongest evidence that I can provide to demonstrate what I've said above is how the meaning process makes us feel. Some readers may be put off by what is essentially a neo-Romantic argument that accents the authority of feelings. But the feelings that are the result of meaning are never divorced from our whole-body activity. The muscle contractions and the immediately following relaxation that comes after solving a major problem, which includes some kind of physical performance, suggests to me that the entire body—the whole self—is impacted by our meaning efforts. The feeling we get when we attain meaning, which always comes in degrees depending on the intensity of what we're trying to solve, is a compression as well as an expansion of our core self. The moment of exuberance and relaxation that comes after executing a musical performance or completing a major athletic feat can be understood as a moment of transcendence, a connection with the wider world, but also immanence, a true grounding in one's humanity.

Holistic Religious Meaning as Peace

Finally, the pursuit of meaning brings serenity, peace of mind. A critical thinker feels unsettled when portions of his or her worldview are disturbed, fractured, or missing. We seek to close such ruptures. God is the ultimate piece in our coherence-seeking life journey. Augustine of Hippo (354-430) confessed that the human heart is restless until it finds rest in God. Ultimate peace can only be achieved when it finds comfort in the Creator. This, of course, does not mean that all the answers are given to us with pristine clarity. The peace that we attain requires faith; indeed, it *is* faith that gives us peace. An important part of the amity that we receive is knowledge of self. Defenders of the liberal arts often talk about a liberal arts education as an opportunity for young people to discover who they are. This is why a consistently Christian perspective is important: knowledge of self requires the knowledge of God. In the opening pages of the *Institutes of the Christian Religion*, John Calvin (1509-1564) proposed that the knowledge of self requires knowledge of God.

"In the first place, no one can look upon himself without turning his thoughts to the contemplation of God, in whom he 'lives and moves' (Acts 17:28)."[10] Accordingly, the knowledge of ourselves not only arouses us to seek God, but also, as it were, leads us by the hand to find him. Again, it is certain that man never achieves a clear knowledge of himself unless he has first looked upon God's face, and then descends from contemplating him to scrutinizing himself.[11]

Without knowledge of God, we have little knowledge of self or world. (Note the relationality between self and world with God.) This is the source of humanity's restless anxiety. The Triune God, who not only allowed Augustine to be freed from his immoral past, was also the missing link that gave him an understanding of his place in the world as being in covenant with God—a peace that passes all understanding. In short, the God piece *is* peace.

Once the human subject turns to God, the creator of all things, then he or she will better understand who they are. God is not simply the depositor of a true knowledge of the world; through Him, our minds come to know, even on an experiential level, the one who providential upholds and sustains the cosmos. When we attain this "genuine self-knowledge," Reformational philosopher Herman Dooyeweerd

(1894-1977) writes, we "draw together the totality of our existence…and focus it upon our authentic, fundamental relationship to God, who is the absolute and single origin and creator of all that is."[12] As Paul writes in Colossians 1:16-18, "all things hold together" in and through Christ and the Spirit. And it requires the work of a transformed mind to draw together into mutual coherence the modal aspects of life, which propels us—from the center of our being—toward intimacy with God.

I need to be careful on this point, however. The liberal arts are often utilized to disrupt our sense of the world, to create cognitive dissonance. What is also clear is that we may not reach a peaceful mind during our four years in college. But this is what should excite us about learning. Instead of demanding answers to the mysteries of life, we should creatively participate in making sense of it all, not arbitrarily, of course, but prayerfully under the guidance of others, especially instructors equipped to show us the path. We also rely on the Holy Spirit, who guides us into all truth. Even then, however, we see the world dimly, yet we rest on the one who creates, maintains, and redeems all things. Our learning journey, which is never ultimately complete in this life, is attached to the Triune God, the source of human fulfillment. It's like raising a child. There is no perfect way of doing it; nonetheless, there is joy in participating in the journey of forming an unbreakable bond that transforms both for the better. Beauty, harmony, and coherence are not dependent on perfection. We can still reach meaningful moments even when certain parts are not fully disclosed.

Each chapter emphasizes the religious nature of higher learning. Chapter one considers one of the leading challenges to achieving a holistic and meaningful learning experience: social media use. The frenetic movement of information and hyperconnectivity have, ironically, made it increasingly difficult to value meaning. This chapter highlights a few of the paradoxes that have significantly impeded the progress of learning.

With the contemporary context in view, chapter two grounds the overall discussion of the liberal arts in a theological tradition. It is my conviction that the Reformed tradition, particularly that which developed from the influence of Calvin and Calvinists like Abraham Kuyper (1837-1920) and Dooyeweerd, the pioneers of Neo-Calvinism and Reformational philosophy respectively, who sought to apply Calvin to the challenges of the modern era, provide the most consistent, coherent, and cogent summary of the sovereignty of God and His work in all of life. The liberal arts provide the best way to understand the integral nature of reality. But without the centrality of God, who creates, upholds, and gives meaning to all things, such an educational pursuit is significantly cut short.

Chapters three through six speak to familiar descriptive features and practices of Christian higher learning. Chapter three examines the faith-integration language prevalent among evangelical institutions. Challenging the idea that faith and learning are somehow separate from one another, this chapter, taking from what has been articulated in the Reformed tradition, reintroduces the idea that faith drives learning.

Chapters four and five consider several leading outcomes shared by Christian colleges and universities—namely, critical thinking and the idea of community. Chapter four incorporates biblical wisdom into discussions on critical thinking, arguing that learning how to live comes from the decisions we make in various social settings. The liberal arts, I contend, allow students to read the world correctly. This includes understanding the diversity of life in order to contribute to the flourishing of that life. Chapter five reminds readers that humans are communal beings and as such must learn in a communal setting. It includes practical suggestions based on best-practices data that will lead to a stronger and more vibrant learning environment.

The final section, chapter six, encourages readers to think about the liberal arts as a spiritual practice. Attending to the world—especially the needs of a fallen world—communing with it, opening oneself up to it, are acts of worship, an education that is deeply spiritual. The final endeavor of this work is to get the reader to meditate on the inescapably religious nature of higher education.

Notes

[1]Michael Roth, *Beyond the University: Why Liberal Education Matters* (New Haven: Yale University Press, 2014), 7.

[2]Albert Einstein, *Ideas and Opinions,* trans. Carl Seelig and ed. Sonja Bargmann (New York: Bonanza Books, 1954), 293.

[3]Andrew Newberg, Eugene d'Aquili, and Vince Rause, *Why God Won't Go Away: Brain Science and the Biology of Belief* (New York: Random House, 2002), 154.

[4]Carol Albright and James Ashbrook, *Where God Lives in the Human Brain* (New York: Sourcebooks, 2001), 13.

[5]Ibid., 15.

[6]Mark William Roche, *Why Choose the Liberal Arts?* (Notre Dame: University of Notre Dame, 2010), 16.

[7]Keat's quote in Fant's *Liberal Arts* (Wheaton: Crossway, 2010), 82.

[8]Harry Stout, ed., *The Writings of Jonathan Edwards* (New Haven: Yale University Press, 2009), 27.

[9]Ibid.

[10]John Calvin, *Institutes of the Christian Religion,* 1:1.

[11]Ibid., 1:1-2

[12]Herman Dooyeweerd, *The Roots of Western Culture: Pagan, Secular, and Christian Options* (Toronto: Wedge Press, 1979), 33.

CHAPTER 1

MEANING IN THE AGE OF INCOHERENCE

In making a case for the inherently religious nature of the liberal arts, it's important to discuss the challenges that such an education faces. While I agree with Roth that liberal arts institutions are "under siege today," I'm not so pessimistic to say, as Victor Ferral does in *Liberal Arts at the Brink*, that they "are in trouble."[1] Essays in leading education and business journals have shown an increasing demand among professionals for liberally trained critical and creative college graduates. What, then, needs to be done to convince the wider world of the importance of the liberal arts and implement real change? One of the biggest challenges that liberal arts advocates face is the conflict between ideological intention and practical action. Liberal arts institutions are competing not with other institutions but with an educational culture that is narrowly specialized and consumer-driven. There is certainly interest in a liberal arts renaissance but very little passion to confront the conditions that have hardened our anti-liberal arts culture. A call for change must include a courageous examination of our habits.

A liberal arts education drives at coherence. The word *cohere* comes from the Latin *co* (together) and *haerere* (to stick). The term, though seemingly redundant, denotes an intense togetherness where separation is veritably impossible, a unity and plurality. The challenge to true coherence today comes from the information economy. Unfortunately, habits produced by a culture shaped by social media make coherence exceedingly difficult—if not altogether obsolete.[2] There is no overarching unity between isolated moments of information on Wikipedia or Twitter, no meaningful relationships created through Facebook, no sustained links in thought when bombarded by online ads. Social media renders incoherent much of life; there is no *mens ex machina*. The fractured mind of the twenty-first century thinks in tweets, hashtags, or oblate to-do lists, and expresses its longings through 140-character techno-grunts. The "flat, featureless, factual" design of the digital age, according to one writer, "sets the standard for intellectual style."[3] Knowledge in a media-based culture is "lost in information," to borrow from T.S. Eliot. Life becomes an array of spasmodic blips. My desire here is not to reject the helpful qualities of social media or to provide a general critique of a consumer or business model-type of education, many intellectuals have addressed these issues, but rather for readers to consider the way in which an obsession with social media has presented considerable challenges for educators and students.

The current age of incoherence—made in part by social media—has produced a handful of paradoxes that cut through all of life, furthering us from deep meaning. The first is the *togetherness-separation* paradox. Through advanced information technology our world is tightly interconnected, yet such global interconnectivity, the latest mode of capitalist development, has further divided peoples and communities, offering only the illusion of community. The "global community" of the twentieth-first century that replaced the "national*isms*" of the nineteenth is far from a "community." We may be able to see political unrest across the world through the media, but we remain separated by coding systems. The world remains divided. On the micro level, family members at home may spend time with each other physically, but they live in their own virtual worlds, separated from one another through the technology that enslaves them.

Since we spend so much time in the virtual, we become unfamiliar with the actual and are, therefore, disconnected from real-life issues. We divorce the real from the virtual, spending more time with the latter, essentially preferring it over the former. We come to value online "friendships" as more real than traditional ones, virtual love as real love. While we may agree that such things are not "really real," we act as if they are. As we intensify the habits of our virtual lives, we increasingly make invisible that which we once took as "the real." Harlan Loeb, professor at Northwestern Law School, writes that social media impairs "our problem solving [*sic*] skills, diminishing meaningful advocacy in the court of public opinion."[4] Consequently, we erase problems, especially social problems, in the virtual worlds we create, developing an inability to deal with real-life challenges. In a neo-Nietzschean sense, the real is dead, and *we* have killed it.

Related to this first paradox is the dilemma of living in a world with greater access to information but very little creative skill to help make sense of the cacophony of isolated wiki-blips, interruptive pop-ads, and ephemeral buzz feeds. Young people have a wealth of information at their finger-

tips, yet they don't know how to process it. As Mark Bauerlein writes in *The Dumbest Generation*, "While the world has
provided [teens and young adults] chances to gain knowledge
and improve their reading/writing skills, not to mention offering financial incentives to do so, young Americans today
are no more learned or skillful than their predecessors, no
more knowledgeable, fluent, up-to-date, or inquisitive, except
in the materials of youth culture. They don't know any more
history or civics, economics or science, literature or current
events."[5] Along these lines, and related to the liberal arts, the
flow of information today has seriously threatened the holistic nature of literacy. First, vocabulary has shrunk significantly in the last decade alone. Not only have we ignored the joy
of meditating on richer or more robust words to communicate deeper meaning, we cannot put what few words we have
together coherently. Social media compresses phrases into
two to four letter acronyms (e.g., LOL, LMAO, BFF, IMO, JK,
NSFW, OMG, TBT, YOLO). Such compression is symptom-
atic of our hyper-democratized consumer culture. Geography,
communities, individuals, and now words take up too much
time and space, the twin foes of modern capitalism.

Second, reading comprehension, an indispensable liberal
arts skill, is cut short. Online readers are relentlessly bombarded by hyperlinks and advertisements that undermine
coherence and greater retention, fracturing thought process-
ing to isolated words and images.[6] Studies have shown that
those who read physical books retain more information than
those reading on a screen.[7] Reading a book is a sensuous experience; it is not only visual but tactile. When we use our
hands to hold open a book, highlight a page, carefully read a
passage with our finger, feel the weight of the book, or even
smell it, we tend to retain much more than when reading on

a computer screen. Our physical and olfactory senses are like the markers we set when hiking a trail; they keep us from getting lost by interconnecting our entire journey. A whole-body reading is an intimate relationship with a book, an experience less meaningful if reading is restricted to sight only.

Third, such habits hold back sustained concentration—concentration that would allow us to make creative arguments. We can share pithy statements on Facebook or Twitter, but the system is set up in such a way that we cannot offer supporting points in order to make a persuasive argument. This has spilled over into the world of public discourse. Listeners are easily swayed by rhetorical riffs rather than rhetorical compositions. The act of "liking" someone's opinions is not all that better, for discussion dissolves "into contests of 'whose side is more popular.'"[8] We may "like" a person's provocative updates, because they accord with our own opinions, but do we really know or can we justify what *we* like or what our virtual "friend" likes. How often do we spend time critically reflecting on the numerous motivational memes we see each day online? No time, no room; so, we move on to the next distracting bombardment in the online grocery story of ideas. A few years ago, a colleague gave a chapel talk on this very issue. At the end of his talk, he invited the audience to spend a couple of minutes in silence. For most of us, myself included, it was highly uncomfortable. Time has become our "frenemy."

The truncation of words, reading, and argumentation is not only a truncation of thinking and meaning but also of the self. As our language becomes bland when under the influence of the cold, static nature of social media, we too become bland and boring, devoid of the creativity essential to critical thinking—and being. Yet we think of ourselves as self-reliant Emersonians who refuse to grope among the "dry bones of the past."[9] We're in control of our own lives, our own choices—so we think. In reality, however, we rarely evaluate the authority or veracity of who or what shapes us with a critical eye. But where do our opinions come from but the inventions we think are simply giving us aid? These inventions do more than provide a service, they think for us. Intelligence is measured by how fast a person in a crowd can Google a question on his or her device, confusing the smartphone with a smart person. Our inventions do for us what we have the responsibility to do as human beings. In short, our creations threaten our creatureliness.

Following the *togetherness-separation* dilemma is the *escapist-enslaving* paradox. Social media offers the means of escape, to tune in *and* tune out, providing unlimited opportunities to take with us the consumer items needed to actualize our escape. Yet this escapism puts us into contact with others who use the same technology as we do and for the same end, becoming zombie consumers with the same loud personalized music, random ringtones, and isolated conversations besmeared with a few distinct yet vague fillers. We may be able to escape for a time, but we're never able to leave, creating the conditions of what Todd Gitlin calls "nomadicity."[10] Ironically, our effort to escape is really a matter of trying to "fit in." The only way out of isolation, we think, is to create our own virtual worlds. There is no learning how to live—no wisdom (see chapter 3)—if we are the sole administrators of our fabricated (read "false") reality.

Finally, the habits of our virtual worlds produce what we might call the moving-isolationism paradox. In our accelerated lives, we find ourselves arrested and suffocating in a sea of information and instant connections. We multitask; we're on the move; we send banal text after banal text; we incessantly check and recheck Facebook feeds, not always realizing we're doing so. But where are we going, and what are we doing in an ultimate sense? These questions are raised when society reaches a critical point. The isolation-movement of social media has, in an important way, profoundly altered our sense of time. In particular, it has brought us closer to the end of generations. This is a difficult—if not troubling—concept to grasp. It's not just the millennials whose minds are increasingly shrinking. Since the Industrial Revolution, time has been one of two central enemies of market capitalism. Time (also space) gets in the way of the accumulation of capital. Today, the speed of social media and all things electronically viral have made life move at such a high speed that generations, according to psychologist Larry Rosen in his book *iDisorder*, are becoming increasingly shorter.[11] This may be a bit modest of Rosen, for we can imagine a point in which time runs backward, swallowing up each extant generation, from the baby boomers to the millennials. What "past" generation will be remembered? I guess we'll just have to Google it. Social media has become a very small baby step forward in the realization of time travel. For example, many baby-boom grandparents, shaped by a technologically advanced world, have been swept up into disintegrated thinking like their millennial grandchildren.

The discussion above speaks to those under the tyranny of social media—how members of society have allowed a human creation to rule over them, perverting the relationship of the Creator with the creation. Thinkers refer to this as "self-alienation." Social media has had a profound impact on the development of the human mind, changing it altogether.[12] Paradoxes paralyze us. How can we overcome the arrested development caused by the dilemmas articulated above? The question is whether a return to the liberal arts can initiate a reform of education? "Today's age," Notre Dame's

Mark Roche argues, "does not easily lend itself to a sense of coherence, but to read great literature and to understand the unfolding narrative of a human life, as well as the developing whole of an artwork, we gain a deeper sense of coherence that is transferable to reflection on ourselves, on the hidden logic of our own development."[13]

A Coherent Mind

By allowing media technology to dictate our lives, we have contributed to the age of incoherence. "A distinguishing characteristic of the modern age," Roche continues, "along with the elevation of instrumental values, is the loss of an organic worldview."[14] The liberal arts provide guidance in understanding our particular situation in the world. James Sire, author of *The Universe Next Door*, argues that a worldview is essentially "a set of presuppositions (assumptions which may be true, partially true or entirely false) which we hold (consciously or subconsciously, consistently or inconsistently) about the basic makeup of our world":

> *What is prime reality—the really real?*
>
> *What is the nature of external reality, that is, the world around us?*
>
> *What is a human being?*
>
> *What happens to persons at death?*
>
> *Why is it possible to know anything at all (are we products of an all-knowing conscious God or the result of evolutionary adaptation)?*
>
> *How do we know what is right or wrong?*
>
> *What is the meaning of human history?*

Sire believes that such questions represent "a fundamental orientation of the heart."[15]

Similarly, in *The Transforming Vision*, authors Brian Walsh and J. Richard Middleton identify "four fundamental" questions universal to all worldviews: "(1) Who am I? Or, what is the nature, task, and purpose of human beings? (2) Where am I? Or, what is the nature of the world and universe I live in? (3) What's wrong? Or, what is the basic problem or obstacle that keeps me from attaining fulfillment? In other words, how do I understand evil? And (4) What is the remedy? Or, how is it possible to overcome this hindrance to my fulfillment? In other words, how do I find salvation?"[16] Answers to these questions are part of a shared human desire for internal stability, "a solution to the riddles of life," Sire writes, "that provides a way of successfully thinking and acting in the world."[17]

The liberal-arts trained student asks the big questions of life—questions related to the place of self in the wider world. Who am I? What's it all about? Is there more than the everyday routine? How might I be fulfilled as a human being? The more diverse coordination of multiple disciplines, the better a student will be able to formulate answers. A question of history will no doubt be helped by philosophy, literature, and art. A theological perspective becomes more acute when it incorporates economics, politics, sociology, and history. A scientist will be a better scientist if he or she is trained in music and poetry. An aspiring writer will become a better writer if he or she is trained to think historically, scientifically, and philosophically. A liberal arts education underscores the importance of how various disciplines (e.g., history, literature, physics, and theology) interact with one another to form a holistic educational experience. The diversity of questions inspired by the liberal arts allows students to make connections with other questions, and the more connected the questions, the deeper a student entrenches him or herself on a quest (where the word question comes from) that traverses the multiple layers of being and meaning.

An education by which the ultimate questions are asked from different disciplinary angles in the pursuit of meaning leads students toward greater coherence, closing what we might call "ignorance gaps." Coherence begins by overcoming a variety of experiential disturbances. On this point, liberal arts educators can benefit tremendously from the work done in the field of neuroscience. None of the works related to building a Christian worldview in the last thirty years have taken into consideration the actual working brain. Of course, it would be unfair to lay blame since neuroscience has made some considerable advances in the last few years alone. But times are changing, and we would do well to reconfigure our approach to worldview. "Any time our left brain is confronted with information that does not jibe with our self-knowledge or conceptual framework," writes Michael Gazzaniga, a leader in the world of neurology and former member of the President's Council on Bioethics, "our left-hemisphere interpreter creates a belief to enable all incoming information to make sense and mesh with our ongoing idea of our self."[18] "The human species is a believing animal," he continues, "searching for order and something to believe in. That is the way our brains work. The interpreter seeks patterns, order, and causal relationships."[19] For a handful of neuroscientists, fractures, gaps, or disconnects in our cognitive and social experiences produce feelings—mild (migraines) to severe (phantom limb pain or the death of a loved one)—of being unsettled, disordering our world, making us restless. Reconciling disturbances in the mind is fundamental to worldview building.

We would come closer to a renaissance of learning if the habits of life mimicked the workings of the brain.[20] The intricate function of the cerebral cortex has been considered the "seat of human nature" whereby we work to arrange the stuff of reality. The brain "requires the coordinated interaction of both sides of the cortex."[21] Cognition cannot be directly pinpointed as a strict "mental process per se but rather a selective combination of these processes that is purposively directed toward effective adaptation."[22] The brain, like the world it perceives, is an integrated system. "Together," writes Andrew Newberg, "these areas of the brain help to provide ourselves with the sense of a rational mind and cohesive understanding of the world around us."[23] I'd like to draw an analogy between the experiences of a disintegrated mind with that of our disintegrated era. When our minds are in disarray, losing the whole picture, we often feel it; that is, the body itself sends signals that something is amiss. "While there is an external reality," Antonio Damasio writes, "what we know of it would come through the agency of the body proper in action, via representations of its perturbations."[24] I'd like to think about how the brain adapts to certain breaches produced in our visual, physical, social, and cultural experiences.

Consider the brain's ability to "fill-in" blind spots. I always know when I'm having a migraine. Jagged veins or spots appear and eventually take up a large portion of my visual plane. This bright branch-like aura is preceded by a major blind spot. But the blind spot is not a matter of "seeing" empty space. "Instead of seeing an enormous void in its place," neuropsychologist V.S. Ramachandran observes, the brain will "fill-in" the blind spot with surrounding colors and objects: "the region corresponding to the missing object is simply covered with the same color of paint or wallpaper."[25] The brain does this automatically. When there is more severe damage to the occipital region, the mind will fill in the blind area with more colorful images, some as odd as cartoon characters.

Similarly, the brain works to fill in the blank physical spaces left by severed limbs. Those with severed limbs often suffer real pain in the empty area. This is due to the fact that the brain cannot reconcile what should be there: an actual limb. The brain recognizes something incomplete. Ramachandran has developed a technique that essentially retrains the brain for phantom-limb pain sufferers. His appropriately designated mirror box, a device whereby an intact limb is reflected in the corresponding mirror at the place of detachment, has allowed phantom limb sufferers to train the brain to "think" there is an attached limb when in fact the person knows better. Ramachandran's aim in these experiments is to suggest that the brain "abhors a vacuum," whether a blind spot or severed limb, "and will apparently supply whatever information is required to complete the scene."[26] When the areas cannot be filled in or are filled with something foreign, the patient is unsatisfied.

Building a holistic world-perspective is not just a matter of attending to the missing pieces in our visual or physical field. Yale University's Bruce Wexler argues that the mind is also engaged in closing social gaps. Consider the readjustments necessary when faced with the loss of a loved one.[27] Losing a spouse is more than emotionally traumatic. The traumatized person, according to Wexler, is often concretely "seeing, hearing, smelling, touching, and being touched by the other person." The "interpersonal sensory environment," which shapes our interpretation of the external world, "is now gone": "The feeling that part of oneself has died is common enough to be one of the diagnostic criteria for pathological grief, *as is the feeling that one's worldview has been shattered.*"[28] The bereaved have experiences of voices and even hallucinations of their lost loved ones. They have also reenacted past conversations and experiences. The loss of a significant other is a kind of double loss. It is not simply the death of another, but a partial, and no less essential, death of the identity of the person still alive. Life with a loved one reorients the brain without our conscious determination. The brain incorporates the person of the other as a result of constant communion, changing thereby the identity of both individuals. When scripture talks about the two individuals become one flesh in the institution of marriage it is not referring simply to a legal or spiritual oneness, but a physical oneness. The couple, over time, literally becomes a two *and* one. And when our loved one is gone, we encounter a new world—one that requires considerable readjustment.

The same unsettling feelings arise when we encounter different cultures, according to Wexler. We tend to associate with the things we are familiar with. Familiarity, of course, requires regular attendance. The brain then becomes comfortable with those parts of life. In the absence of cultural familiarity, however, the brain is troubled and pursues a course of adjustment. As Wexler suggests, we tend to associate with shared cultural characteristics. Culture links us to others, forming thereby a communal identity. Consider the non-life-threatening situation of being in a social context in which our native language is not a part. We feel disconnected. But the perturbation caused by our disconnection begins to dissipate when we hear just one person speaking our own language. In fact, such a person could be standing across a room. Over time we grow accustomed to our cultural habits; breaking those habits can often be difficult. We don't always welcome new experiences that unsettle our familiar habits. Consider the manner by which we create racial stereotypes. "If you've had a bad experience with a member of a minority group—or even just heard or read something unfavorable about the group—it's only too easy to react prejudicially toward a member of that group."[29] Our own cultural disturbance can result in social conflict. "The successful restoration of harmony," key to worldview structuring and body consonance, "requires the systematic and thorough restructuring of the inner world to match the now-altered outer world."[30] We must be open to the many surprises that may potentially unsettle our familiar experience. This openness, as we'll see in a later chapter, is a key aspect of wisdom. The liberal arts allow students to become familiar with the history, literature, and art of a host of different communities. This equips them to handle a number of unanticipated experiences.

A contemporary revival of learning should include a change in both thoughts and habits. I want to avoid presenting myself as some kind of modern-day Luddite, but I think a little aggression in confronting our age of incoherence might be healthy. Given our (hyper)information age, which discourages contemplation for the sake of deeper meaning, higher education has rejected the value of struggling with higher-order questions, largely because such questions take time and time is the one thing we have very little of. If there is no time, there is no education. The word *school* comes from the Latin *scola,* which in turn "derives from the Greek term for leisure (*schole*)."[31] It's not that the current mode of global capitalism, information capitalism, rejects truth, but rather it doesn't have time for it, no time to reflect on what is true, good, and beautiful. The tyranny of the immediate and the commercialization of the fleeting, reflecting habits humans have succumbed to by enslaving themselves to their own creations, are what increasingly make our world incoherent. This culture of fragmentation, Stratford Caldecott writes, "is a denial of ultimate meaning. Contemporary education, therefore, tends to the *elimination of meaning*—except in the sense of a meaning that we impose by force upon the world."[32] The first step in creating a liberal arts renaissance is the simple fortitude to disconnect.

Taking the time to *see* God's creation—to meditate on what is the good, the true, and the beautiful—is to encounter God's communication to us. As Edwards writes,

> [T]he Son of God created the world for his very end, to communicate himself in an image of his own excellency. He communicates himself properly only to spirits; and they only are capable of being proper images of his excellency, for they only are properly beings...Yet he communicates a sort of shadow or glimpse of his excellencies to bodies, which, as we have shown, are but the shadows of being, and not real beings...So the green trees and fields, and singing of birds, are the emanations of his infinite joy and benignity; the easiness and naturalness of trees and vines [are] shadows of his infinite beauty and loveliness; the crystal rivers and murmuring streams have the footsteps of his sweet grace and bounty.[33]

The allusiveness of God's communication is not an excuse to abandon a clear knowledge of the one communicating. No excuse exists for unbelief. Indeed, I believe that we'd lose the beauty of such divine speech in creation if it were explicit. Instead, we should consider the exciting opportunity to revel in God's richly oblique revelation like a lover with a betrothed.

Notes

[1] Victor Ferral, *Liberal Arts at the Brink* (Cambridge: Harvard University Press, 2011), 3.

[2] This is not to reject the many positive aspects of social media. But when highlighting the positive we tend to ignore the negative. All of creation is subject to the fall. There is nothing more consistently egalitarian than sin and death. God's creation has been subjected to the curse. What is more, the things created by humans are also subject to the fall. To ignore the fallenness even in the good things that we make is to reduce such creations to an idol. Debating the pros and cons of the information age should be done in another setting. But there is something that we can agree on: information technology and the habits it imposes on us have made a defense of the liberal arts increasingly difficult.

[3] Mark Bauerlein, *The Dumbest Generation: How the Digital Age Stupefies Young Americans and Jeopardizes Our Future* (New York: Tarcher/Penguin Books, 2009), 153.

[4] www.huffingtonpost.com/harlan-loeb/critical-thinking-social-media_b_4528125.html.

[5] Bauerlein, *Dumbest Generation,* 9.

[6] Nicholas Carr, *The Shallows: What the Internet is Doing to Our Brains* (New York: W.W. Norton & Co., 2010), 129.

[7] http://www.scientificamerican.com/article/reading-paper-screens/.

[8] Ibid., 129.

[9] Ralph Waldo Emerson, "Nature" in *The Essential Writings of Ralph Waldo Emerson* (New York: Random House, 2000), 3.

[10] Todd Gitlin, *Media Unlimited: How the Torrent of Images and Sounds Overwhelms our Lives* (New York: Picador, 2007), 55.

[11] Larry Rosen, *iDisorder: Understanding our Obsession with Technology and Overcoming its Hold on Us* (New York: St. Martin's, 2012). https://www.psychologytoday.com/blog/rewired-the-psychology-technology/201003/welcome-the-igeneration.

[12] Carr, *The Shallows.*

[13] Mark William Roche, *Why Choose the Liberal Arts?* (Indiana: University of Notre Dame, 2010), 139.

[14] Roche, *Why Liberal Arts,* 130.

[15] James Sire, *The Universe Next Door,* 5th ed. (Downers Grove: InterVarsity Press, 2009), 13, 19-20.

[16] Brian Walsh and J.Richard Middleton, *The Transforming Vision: Shaping a Christian Worldview* (Downers Grove: InterVarsity Press, 1984), 35.

[17] James Sire, *Naming the Elephant: Worldview as a Concept* (Downers Grove: InterVarsity Press, 2009), 26. Furthermore, a worldview need not be explicitly worked out in exact detail according to James Olthius. See Olthius, "On Worldviews" *Christian Scholars Review* 14 (1985): "A worldview (or vision of life) is a framework or set of fundamental beliefs through which we view the world and our calling and future in it. This vision need not be fully articulated: it may be so internalized that it goes largely unquestioned; it may not be explicitly developed into a systematic conception of life; it may not be theoretically deepened into a philosophy; it may not even be codified into a creedal form; it may be greatly refined through cultural-historical development. Nevertheless, this vision is a channel for the ultimate beliefs which give direction and meaning to life. It is the integrative and interpretative framework by which order and disorder are judged; it is the standard by which reality is managed and pursued; it is the set of hinges on which all our everyday thinking and doing turns." See also Albert Wolters, *Creation Regained: Biblical Basics for a Christian Worldview* (Grand Rapids: Eerdmans, 1985) and Michael Goheen and Craig Bartholomew, *Living at the Crossroads: An Introduction to Worldview* (Grand Rapids: Baker Academic, 2009). Chapter 3 will offer more on this note.

[18] Michael Gazzaniga, *The Ethical Brain: The Science of Our Moral Dilemmas* (New York: Harper Perennial, 2005), 151. The majority of neuroscientists adopt an evolutionary perspective regarding the origins of the religious and worldview functioning brain. This study

is not interested in entering the creation-evolution debate, although it does presuppose the former as a starting point.

[19]Ibid., xviii.

[20]Andrew Newberg, Eugene d'Aquili, and Vince Rause's outline of the brain in *Why God Won't Go Away: Brain Science and the Biology of Belief* is perhaps one of the clearest. The temporal lobe, located at the immediate base of the brain stem, is the area associated with language, memory, and conceptual thought. Above the temporal is the frontal lobe, which takes up a large portion of the top-front of the brain, deals with attention (reasoning, including problem solving) and muscle activity. The ability to see comes from the occipital lobe, across from the temporal lobe. Finally, the parietal lobe, between the frontal and occipital and above the temporal, is responsible for sense perception as well as visual and body orientation. The cerebellum, the little brain at the base of the occipital and temporal lobes, helps regulate movement and balance.

Here is another explanation of the key association areas of the brain. The first, the orientation association area, "situated at the posterior section of the parietal lobe, receives sensory input from the sense of touch as well as from other sensory modalities, especially vision and hearing. These give it the ability to create a three-dimensional sense of 'body' and to orient that body in space" (28). Playing "a major role in governing complex, integrated bodily movements and behaviors associated with attaining goals," is the prefrontal cortex, producing the attention association area: "this area helps the body organize the behaviors necessary for reaching desired objects of moving toward some chosen destination" (29). The attention association area allows us to focus on an object or idea. Finally, the verbal conceptual area, "located at the junction of the temporal, parietal, and occipital lobes, is primarily responsible for generating abstract concepts and for relating those concepts to words…the comparison of concepts, the ordering of opposites, the naming of objects and categories of objects, and the high-order grammatical and logical functions." The inner workings of the verbal conceptual area develop consciousness "and the expression of consciousness through language" (31).

[21] Ibid.

[22] *Britannica Guide to the Brain: A Guided Tour of the Brain—Mind, Memory, and Intelligence*, introduction by Cordelia Fine (London: Constable and Robinson, 2008), 21.

[23] Newberg, *Principles of Neurotheology*, 73.

[24] Antonio Damasio, *Descartes' Error* (New York: Penguin Books, 1994), 235.

[25] Ramachandran and Blakeslee, *Phantoms in the Brain* (New York: HarperCollins, 1998), 89.

[26] Ibid.

[27] Bruce E. Wexler, *Brain and Culture* (Cambridge: MIT Press, 2006), 5.

[28] Ibid.

[29] Richard Restak, *The Naked Brain* (New York: Three Rivers Press, 2007), 83.

[30] Bruce E. Wexler, *Brain and Culture* (Cambridge: MIT Press, 2006), 172-73.

[31] Roche, *Why Liberal Arts*, 27.

[32] Stratford Caldecott, *Beauty for Truth's Sake: On the Re-enchantment of Education* (Grand Rapids: Brazos Press, 2009), 17.

[33] *The Works of Jonathan Edwards* (New Haven: Yale University Press, 1957-2008), 13:279.

CHAPTER 2

REFORMED LIBERAL ARTS

The western world has been profoundly shaped by the six-teenth-century Protestant Reformation. The Reformation confronted arbitrary power and widespread ignorance, helped in part to give rise to the revolutionary age, create that lofty, yet somewhat nebulous, political entity we call "the people," and nurture the ideological conditions for modern capitalism and the modern state. These developments were largely unintentional, for the magisterial Reformers were centrally concerned with doctrine. The Reformation was a historical "recovering" of biblical theology, a "return to the beliefs and practices of the early church."[1] For more than a century and a half prior to Martin Luther igniting the Reformation by posting the *Ninety-Five Theses* to the church door at Wittenberg on October 31, 1517, pre-modern Europe was in shambles, having just barely recovered from a devastating plague and a major war under a church weakened by its own internal

problems—not least of these included political factions, nep-
otism, insatiable greed, and widespread ignorance.[2] By 1517,
the conditions were ripe for reform.

A number of historical factors motivated the Reformation.
One very important cause was the recovery of the humanities
during the historical period known as the Renaissance. "Renaissance humanism was widely regarded as providential, in
that the great advances made in Hebrew and Greek studies
in relation to classical texts in western Europe paved the way
for the direct engagement with the scriptural text, in place
of the unreliable Latin translation of the Vulgate."[3] Liberally
educated thinkers like Martin Luther, John Calvin, and Ul-
rich Zwingli applied their learning to the reading of ancient
texts, especially the Bible, and came to the conclusion that
the gospel had been lost—or suppressed—by the very powerful Roman Catholic Church. It is hard to imagine whether
a reformation of the church would have occurred at the time
that it did had it not been for the Renaissance. The strength
of a theologically robust faith tradition is threatened when
learning is significantly undervalued.

There is no doubting the role of higher learning in creating the Protestant Reformation. There is also no doubt of the
Reformation's continuing influence on higher education into
the modern age. This is not to say that other faith traditions
have failed when it comes to education. Indeed, it seems that
the strength of faith is reinforced by a strong education. In
its intent to provide a radically biblical approach to all of life,
fundamentally reshaping our perspective on the world, the
Reformation had a profound impact on education. We grow
as the heart is guided to study God's word, which then directs
our entire lives. And we continue to grow in the way the Holy
Spirit guides in truth, a divinely embedded education. Faith
without knowledge and instruction is dead. Within the last

four decades, in fact, Christian intellectuals have relied heavily on the influence of Reformed thinkers since the sixteenth century in developing a strong connection between faith and learning. But such a relationship has not always been consistently maintained, theoretically or practically.

Reformed

The contemporary church is replete with those who call themselves "reformed." The emergence of "New Calvinism" in the last few years, for instance, speaks to the increasing interest in the Reformed faith, especially as it relates to salvation. Yet quite often little is known of the faith heritage in which members find themselves. When asked about the meaning of *Reformed,* many within the Reformed community, in fact, rely on the now-familiar maxim "Reformed and always reforming." This is far from a clear definition related to identity, however; it underscores the doing, not the being. It's like defining a horse by saying that "a horse is a horse, of course, of course." What is more, such a vacuous bumper-sticker slogan can be distorted by the democratized consumer culture characteristic of American evangelicalism—the symptoms of which include a quickly evolving boredom with traditional confessional parameters. An Americanized notion of "reforming," in short, tends to become a euphemism for seeker-friendly ecclesial attractions.

My language is particular, but I wish to speak to a general audience. In other words, I'm not proposing a Reformed approach to education in order to divide. Instead, I wish to employ the most biblically consistent language to articulate Christian higher education. The Reformed tradition, which has played a critical role in the history of higher education throughout the western world, provides the language to do just that. If we were to offer a single word—if a single word is possible—to capture the meaning of *Reformed* it would be "sovereignty." Sovereignty means rule or power over. As it applies to salvation, paramount in the minds of the Reformers and the central "hub" of Reformed theology, the word means, as William Edgar points out, that "Salvation belongs to the Lord" (Psalm 3:8). The sovereignty of God's salvation, His grace in saving sinners, is connected to God's justice. The Reformers wrestled with what it meant to be made right before God. Martin Luther, for instance, worked so very hard to please God, to earn God's favor, in order to become righteous. Few could parallel his impeccable piety. But his law-keeping only revealed how much he fell short. Indeed, his so-called works of righteousness only added to his condemnation, until the day he realized that what it meant to be made right before God was a resting and trusting in the perfect work of Christ in His life, His death, and His resurrection.

For believers, then and now, *right-ness* is an imputation (giving over or attributing to another) of the righteousness of Christ through faith alone and for the glory of God alone. This was Luther's moment of enlightenment—a moment that required critical reflection on the scriptures. What joy he and hundreds of others had in knowing that salvation had been achieved by another.

God is absolutely sovereign over salvation as well as creation. This speaks to education in general. Studying creation requires submission to the Creator. Concurrently, both the liberal arts and a recognition of the sovereignty of God share a similar end—freedom. Truth, indeed, not only sets us free, but it also opens up the world. As the rebirth of learning brought intellectual, social, economic, political, and (even) geographical liberation, the Reformation brought spiritual liberation. God's story of salvation as it is revealed to us in the scriptures is a story of ultimate freedom. Freedom comes only when God, through His appointed servant, breaks the bondage of sin and death. This is the nature of grace, an undeserved loving act on the part of God to condescend and make righteous through Christ a people that He calls His own. We are freed *from* the world, the flesh, and the devil *in order to* worship God in the manner in which He requires. Submission to the authority of God allows us to better understand creation, which also has a liberating component.

God's Self-Revelation

At the center of Reformed theology is God's "comprehensive plan of redemption," Edgar highlights, but it's also about God's sovereignty over "*all* good things."[4] Everything that is good, true, and beautiful is a communication of the Spirit, a communication of the light of Christ (Ephesians 5:8-9). God reveals himself in two ways. Special revelation is specific in that it shows, to adopt the *Westminster Shorter Catechism*, what humans are to believe concerning God, and what God requires of humans. As demonstrated in the history of redemption, God used a variety of means to communicate salvation to His people.

The current mode of God's redemptive message is found in the pages of the Old and New Testament, the only infallible standard for faith and practice. The basic story in the Bible is simple. God created a good, sinless world, putting man in charge of tending that world. But because of the disobedience of one man, all of humanity fell into sin, cursing the entire cosmos. God required restitution of His creation. In the course of time, He sent His unique, one-and-only Son to become fully man in order to accomplish and apply redemption—now and in the future—to creation. The entire creation groans—even among the elect of creation—and awaits the consummation of salvation in the new heavens and new earth.

Special revelation centers on redemption and only partially on issues like the human condition outside of redemption. But such matters can be discerned by relying on God's second mode of self-revelation. The revival of both theology and the humanities that came as a result of the Renaissance and Reformation generated a renewed interest in the created order. Many saw the world with new eyes, reinvigorating the doctrine of God's general revelation. As intellectuals saw the world anew, they were introduced to their own knowledge of the Creator. God's authorship, along with His divine attributes, are clearly seen through the things He has made—i.e., *all* of creation. Humans have a moral obligation to recognize and submit to God as they ponder the works of His hands, His poetry. While it may cause us to grow in the knowledge of God, the study of mathematics, for instance, is *not* a means of special grace. In order to grow in the gracious work of sanctification we must attend to the elements of grace put forth in the scriptures. This needs to be understood. But this does not negate the reality that mathematics, given the direction of the heart, is an important communication of God's person.

Readers might be taken aback by that last sentence. Allow me to make a few points of clarification. First, God's special revelation—His message of redemption—comes through general revelation. The (special) message of salvation has been written down by men in specific historical settings (general)—conditions unique to each writer. Thus, we need to make clear that general and special revelation are not sealed off from one another. Second, there is indeed a distinction between the two modes of revelation, but we should never neglect the common link: God's revelation of Himself.

Given our intent to understand Reformed liberal arts better, we should emphasize the fact that all things are created, upheld, and given meaning in and through the divine *Logos,* the second person of the Trinity, and that the good things that students study are communications from God. There is no part of creation where God cannot be seen. We may not be able to see immediately or even completely the divine, but we know He has revealed Himself. Discerning God in the things that are made is akin to looking at the art of Michelangelo, Courbet, or Picasso. We all recognize the work of such masters as beautiful (or we should), but the beauty may not be immediately apparent. It takes work on our part to see not only the beauty in the work but also the beauty of the master. If this is true of human art, how much more the magnificent artistry of God? Students often inquire about the value of studying various subjects (e.g., mathematics, history, music, etc.). My response to students who inquire as to why they need to engage a variety of subjects is that it affords them the opportunity to see what aspect of God's being can be discerned in what they're studying.

Third, unlike the special revelation, general revelation is *not* a closed canon. The scriptures show us that the way of salvation is restricted to the work of Christ. There is no other way to God but through His son, and there is no other way to know this than through his special revelation. Yet there are very few restrictions in the use of our critical and creative imagination to explore God's world. Of course, we are directed to examine the cosmos with godly wisdom—a deep reverence for God—which includes a love for God and neighbor. But there is more to creation that can be revealed—new discoveries, new arguments, new methodologies, new art forms, etc. Humans, as part of the ongoing cultural mandate, have been invited by God to discover the depths and richness of

His creation. This does not mean that the truths in creation can somehow be relativized. God has set the earth in order, but it does not follow that we have fully plumbed the depths of the creation. Humanity has merely scratched the surface.

The church has always affirmed these two ways of communicating, but evangelicals have often muted one (general revelation) by elevating the other (special revelation). By the early twentieth century, notwithstanding the great influence of the First and, especially, Second Great Awakenings, a kind of "Bible only" disposition hardened in the evangelical mind. Such a biblicism intensified the dichotomy between faith and learning, which is discussed in the next chapter. In my brief experience as a college professor, I've noticed how some students attend a Christian college in order to study the Bible— to study the Bible *alone*. All other subjects outside theological studies, many a fallow mind assumes, are unnecessary for Christian maturity. But focusing solely on biblical studies, especially for the purposes of going on to do even more biblical studies at the seminary level, is, from the vantage point of the liberal arts, a very expensive education in redundancy.

Some will protest: "What's wrong with studying the Bible? I just want to learn more about God." Putting aside the sententiousness of such a comment as well as the assumption that directing a more balanced educational experience leads us further away from God and is, therefore, somehow "wrong," the comment presupposes that the best way—or only way—to know God is by studying the Bible and nothing else. Yet the sad reality is that the contemporary pietist who wants only the Bible and refuses—or rejects outright—subjects that articulate the riches of general revelation relegates, in essence, an important part of God's self-revelation. An individual who says that they do not need art or economics, or any other subject, unwittingly ignores the opportunity to consider how God might be revealing Himself through these disciplines. This is a shade of foolishness that comports with minimalist market fundamentalism. In truth, such an attitude reflects an intense self-centeredness. I'm not saying, however, that believers are required to study everything, if that is even possible. I'm simply addressing a flawed approach to Christian learning: a consumer-fundamentalist mindset that rejects the importance of certain subjects—or true learning itself—because they supposedly have little or nothing at all to do with personal salvation. Again, humans pursue salvation and creation in order to know God, which in turn provides knowledge of salvation and creation.

I would suggest that a better understanding of God—his person, work, and world—will come when we study the humanities, the arts, and the sciences in the light of His word. In the end, a dismissive student of either the Bible or non-Bible-specific subjects will cut short a holistic and, therefore, spiritually rich education. Practically speaking, a liberal arts education will increase the ministerial effectiveness of those who eventually find work in the institutional church. As Arthur Holmes writes, "The minister and missionary need a great deal more than a knowledge of Scripture, the habit of prayer, and a way with people and words: they need an understanding of human beings and cultures and socioeconomic problems that is enriched by the social sciences and humanities, and the kind of insight philosophy can give into beliefs other than their own."[5] Believers will grow in their knowledge and love for God and neighbor when they study Moses and Milton, David and Dickens, Paul and Plato. The liberal arts trace out a path to explore God's revelation in greater depth.

Critical Creative Citizens

The origin of the liberal arts can be traced back to ancient Greece, beginning with the polemics of Socrates and Plato, both of whom stressed that the pursuit of knowledge was itself a pursuit of knowing one's self, later to the court under

Charlemagne in the ninth century, and finally to the High Middle Ages, where learning was advanced at universities in Bologna, Paris, and Oxford, and at monasteries at Chartres and Notre Dame. The pedagogical intent was to fashion the whole person—body and soul, head, hands, and heart. And keep in mind that this was not limited to pre-modern Europe. The Muslim world likewise played an important part. Schools established in Alexandria and Baghdad not only collected but also translated and interpreted ancient texts. Contributions from Christian, Muslim, and Jewish scholars during the Middle Ages laid the "foundation of the modern world."[6]

By the time of the Middle Ages, maturing in the line of Greco-Roman thought and culture, the liberal arts curriculum was organized under two branches: the *trivium* and *quadrivium*. The *trivium* consisted of grammar, dialectic (or logic), and rhetoric; the *quadrivium* consisted of arithmetic, geometry, arts, and astronomy. Grammar demonstrated the functional elements of writing; logic, the proper relation between well-formulated propositions for argumentation; and rhetoric, the creative means by which we persuade. Notice how this was all an integrated economy ("economy" comes from the Greek *oikos*, which means household); grammar, logic, and rhetoric are siblings that cannot live apart. The *trivium*, we could say, focused on the universals of writing, reasoning, and communicating for the *individual*. Arithmetic, housed in the *quadrivium*, demonstrated the relation between numbers. Geometry, like logic, encouraged proofs of the mathematical structure of space (distinct but not totally separated from its counterpart, logic, which deals with the mathematics of argumentation). Art showed the arithmetic of imagination. All the things associated with art proper (e.g., music, dance, painting, drama, etc.) have a mathematical structure to them. Finally, unlike all the other disciplines which focus largely on the mind and the structure of the physical earth, astronomy considered the arithmetic of the heavens. These branches of learning served as the foundation for the liberal arts.

What is meant specifically by the liberal arts? The word liberal comes from *liber,* meaning "free" or "to be free." But what is lost in the world of contemporary education is the fact that one must work to acquire that freedom. The *artes* in liberal arts refers to the skills needed to reach that freedom. The question that one may ask is, "What do we mean by freedom?" It is a freedom that is both *from* and *to.* On the one hand, such an education frees us from ignorance. It allows us to challenge systems of power that might keep us in ignorance. In this way, we are liberated from error in order to pursue truth. We also become very powerful agents in the preservation of truth. A text that I have students read in my United States survey course is Frederick Douglass's *Narrative,* a story of Douglass's life as a slave and his successful journey toward freedom in nineteenth-century America. The primary means by which Douglass achieved his liberty was through learning how to read and write. Literacy gave Douglass the ability to understand himself (his status as a slave) and the world around him (the evils of slavery), which in turn helped in his ultimately successful path toward freedom.

Liberal arts advocates push for an education that helps shape the whole person, positioning him or her as part of a larger and richer cosmic mosaic. But let me sharpen this a bit. The goal of a *Christian* liberal arts education is to produce what I call *critical creative citizens* (the "3Cs")—young men and women who confidently engage the world in order to work toward a society in harmony with God's good creational order. Each of the 3Cs are interconnected, and align with the biblical doctrine of the cultural mandate found in Genesis 1:26.[7] Humanity has been given the responsibility not only to fill and subdue but also to cultivate the creation. This is both indicative and imperative. The mandate reflects who we are as human beings, and who we are as image bearers. We cannot help but be creators. It is a moral directive given to humanity by God, a responsibility to tend to the needs of creation. The cultural mandate, in its critical aspect, includes the responsibility to read critically in order to understand God's world, which draws us closer to Him and His creation. For Christians, this certainly means humbly interpreting God's world aright, to submit to its law-order and live accordingly, and to "organize ideas into an ordered whole, to be systematic," Holmes writes, "to work toward a unified understanding."[8] This requires creativity, which is the activity of materializing the critical. As image bearers, humans are fundamentally *creative* agents, cultivating their humanity *by* creating. It's not that we create out of nothing, but, rather, we create (i.e., develop) from what God has graciously given to us.

Critical begins with reading, seeing, and listening to our surroundings. Another way of saying it is that the critical mind is a submissive one. We need to understand creation on the Creator's terms. The contours of those terms are not always clear, hence the reason to engage. At any rate, reading, a woefully deficient skill these days, requires more than understanding the "letter." Higher-level reading moves beyond the embodied discourse to make more intricate connections for greater depth. The great Transcendentalist Henry David Thoreau understood the training needed to learn how to read. He writes in *Walden,* "To read well...is a noble exercise, and one that will task the reader more than any exercise which the customs of the day esteem. It requires a training such as the athletes underwent, the steady intention almost of the whole life to the object."

An important element in reading or paying attention to the world is listening. Listening is not only focused attention but also affectionate caring for the needs of the world. This critical reflection on that which is outside the limits of the self demands creative imagination. "Critical thinking is sterile," Michael Roth writes, "without the capacity for empathy and comprehension that stretches the self."[9] Humans are made to connect with the moods, feelings, and thoughts of others. Empathy leads to us to preserve or change in the way we live.

The *creative* is stimulated when we find ways to explain what we see and read. The intent of the creative is to communicate not *what* we understand, but to communicate *in order to* understand. One way of doing this is through writing, yet another woefully deficient skill in education today. As the Irish poet Cecil Day Lewis wrote in 1951: "We do not write in order to be understood; we write in order to understand."[10] And to add weight and longevity to our creative constructions, we must broaden the aesthetics of our prose. Students need to study not just the rules of grammar and punctuation. In order to find their own voice, they must become, to borrow from George Trevelyan (1876-1962), a "faithful apprentice" of great literature.[11] And what constitutes great literature? Compositions that cannot be removed without the tearing of flesh.

The skill of making an argument in turn demonstrates how the critical and creative come together. We first need to understand an argument before we can develop our own. At the very minimum, an argument is composed of two or more sentences: a major claim with supporting statements. If I make a claim about the world, I must offer subordinate statements to strengthen that claim. When making an assertion, one must always anticipate the "why" question. Answers to the why are the supports to the major claim. We can list the numerous deductive (e.g., *modus ponens* or *modus tollens*) and inductive fallacies (e.g., poor generalizations, begging the question, *ad hominems*, or slippery slopes) presented in a standard logic class. Along with the knowledge of how an argument works, students need to be taught how to construct and communicate arguments effectively. This, once again, returns us to the creative. Students learn words and become adept readers, identifying the structure of a form of literature. They also come to recognize different modes of speaking and writing.

Critical is also associated with the conclusions (arguments or positions) drawn from what we quietly experience. What is the goal of argumentation? First, an argument should be made to elevate truth. We certainly have the tendency to make petty or self-serving arguments. I'm not interested in countering such puerility at this stage. I'm more interested in supporting arguments that contribute to the flourishing of life. We often make counter arguments either to challenge what we may see as a weak argument or an outright false one, exposing oppressive power. Such arguments are advanced for the well-being of others and the world.

Second, an argument is advanced in order to persuade. This links argumentation to rhetoric, the *critical* to the *creative*. No one who has ever made an argument has put aside their creativity. We must not underestimate the *art*—the creating out of nothing—in the art of persuasion. A beautiful argument is one that deeply penetrates because of its overall balance and proportion. We see the order and balance of it (though we may not always accept it). But the artistry behind the argument presupposes an active artist.

Critical and creative skills—hardly exhausted in the above descriptions—require practice and patience. Good reading and writing take time. Again, Trevelyan notes that clarity in writing "is invariably the result of hard labor, and the easily flowing connection of sentence with sentence and paragraph with paragraph has always been won by the sweat of the brow."[12] I can instruct students on how to write a sentence, formulate an argument, use supporting evidence, and consider modes of persuasion, but the student must employ such instruction and practice, practice, practice—until they "get it." (And "getting it," by the way, is not the end. Once a student grasps a particular skill, he or she can become even better.) And the instructor must come alongside the student's habits, to adjust and sharpen the skills process. A coach can articulate the rules of a game and how to play, but it will not catch-on until the player first submits to instruction and practices (this touches the issue of critical wisdom discussed in Chapter 3). And when a young athlete includes in his or her practice a diversity of sports the more he or she will understand the nature—or spirit—of sports *in general*. The skill and content related to knowledge seep into our bodies as we practice. And as we'll see in last chapter, such in-dwelling practices transform us.

Critical and creative thinking helps learners go beyond the immediate or ephemeral, doing so by making numerous connections with the parts encountered in experience. That which is "more real" or "more accurate" in relation to degrees of certainty, what Alvin Plantinga calls "warrant," is drawn out in the things that are complex or, as I like to say to students, in "the fuzzy." A single-line circle that I draw on the whiteboard is less accurate (or true) than a multiple-line circle (hence overlapping circles in one) drawn on the board. The reason is that the mind participates in creating a single line. If the line is off, so is the image of the circle. But the circle becomes increasingly clear when the eye focuses the multiple lines in order to intuit—only in the mind—a more perfect circle. But the more perfect circle requires multiple lines and numerous strokes of the arm and the pen. This analogy works well, I think, in describing the liberal arts. We need multiple subjects—multiple lines—to get a better, more complete picture in our minds of how the world works. The eye is drawn to the many that makes up the one. When we pull together multiple lines—subjects, authorities, concepts, directions, etc.—we piece together clearer images of the world.

Convincing a person of the value of a liberal arts education pivots on answering one—if not *the*—dominant question: "What can a person do with such an education?" While I think this is an appropriate question of stewardship, it is unfortunate that the answer betrays the very *raison d'etre* of the liberal arts. Many are concerned not about self, God, or the wider world, but with whether they can get that one job from that one particular major in order to make a comfortable living. (Recall the student in the introduction.) My clunky answer to this question—and I've been asked quite a few times—is "what can you *not* do with this type of education?" The liberal arts will open up a person's vocational horizons.

Martin Luther once expressed his deep appreciation for the liberal arts because they make a student "fit for everything."[13] Employers value higher-level thinkers and effective communicators.[14] In the contemporary world, students (and parents) need to abandon the assumption that that particular major will provide that one particular job. The narrow rationalism of the contemporary world should compel us to think bigger. A liberal education prepares students for a lifetime of jobs.

If we are committed to a decidedly Christian education, we need to look beyond immediate monetary utility. Training to think critically and creatively is preparation for life, preparation for valuable citizenship. "[T]he ultimate purpose of a liberal arts education," according William Deresiewicz, author of *Excellent Sheep*, "is to help [students] to reflect in the widest and deepest sense, beyond the requirements of work and career: for the sake of citizenship, for the sake of living well with others, above all, for the sake of building a self that is strong and creative and free."[15] In her widely-read *Not for Profit*, Martha Nussbaum reminds readers that early liberal education was valued for the sake of creating "informed, independent, and sympathetic" thinkers—citizens who would be able to "think for themselves, criticize tradition, and understand the significance of another person's sufferings and achievements."[16] We not only become better employees, but better spouses, parents, neighbors, and friends through the liberal arts.

A young individual equipped with a biblical liberal arts education is positioned well to act in a more humane and loving way toward the world and thus have a more positive impact locally and globally. This is the consequence of sharpened critical and creative skills. But I need to offer one last caveat: such a *shalomic* consequence born of these skills does not happen automatically. There are plenty of critical and creative individuals in our world today who have used their skills not for good but for ill, pursuing their own interests at the expense of others. This is where a Christian approach to the liberal arts is of the highest value. The Christian liberal arts college should rest on the foundation of biblical wisdom. We should not pursue higher education for selfish gain. Educating ourselves for selfish (strictly monetary) reasons keeps us from human flourishing; it also furthers us away from our Creator. Critical and creative thinking must be directed toward the other. Educators should encourage students to engage the world in order to enhance their love of God and cultivate, out of a divine love, the well-being of that world. Attaining one's purpose or meaning in life comes from this dynamic love. Christ called His disciples to be witnesses of the gospel to *all* of creation (Mark 16:15)—a creation that "groans" and awaits the consummation (Romans 8). Reconciliation to the Father through the redemptive work of Christ has made Christians ministers of reconciliation. Indeed, it is in the process of serving others—listening, learning, and tending to penultimate and ultimate needs—that we come to discover our own self.

Notes

[1] Alistair McGrath, *Reformation Thought: An Introduction,* 2nd ed. (Hoboken: Wiley-Blackwell, 1993), 21.

[2] William Edgar, *Truth in All its Glory: Commending the Reformed Faith* (Phillipsburg: P&R Publishing, 2001), 39.

[3] McGrath, *Reformation Thought,* 22.

[4] Edgar, *Truth,* 18-19. Emphasis mine.

[5] Arthur Holmes, *The Idea of a Christian College* (Grand Rapids: Eerdmans, 1975), 40.

[6] Stratford Caldecott, *Beauty for Truth's Sake: On the Re-enchantment of Education* (Grand Rapids: Brazos, 2009), 26.

[7] Todd C. Ream and Perry L. Glanzer, *The Idea of a Christian College: A Reexamination for Today's University* (Eugene: Cascade, 2013), 70.

[8] Arthur Holmes, *The Idea of a Christian College* (Grand Rapids: Eerdmans, 1975), 30.

[9] Michael Roth, *Beyond the University: Why Liberal Education Matters* (New Haven: Yale University Press, 2015), 184.

[10] C. Day Lewis, *The Poet's Task: An Inaugural Lecture Delivered Before the University of Oxford* (Oxford: Clarendon Press, 1951), 15.

[11] George Trevelyan, "Cio Rediscovered" in Fritz Stern, ed., *The Varieties of History: From Voltaire to the Present* (New York: Vintage Books, 1973), 239.

[12] Ibid., 240.

[13] Martin Luther, "To the Councilmen of All Cities in Germany that They Establish and Maintain Christian Schools," https://archive.org/details/worksofmartinlut01luth.

[14] http://upstart.bizjournals.com/news/wire/2012/05/14/survey-on-millennial-hiring-highlights-power-of-liberal-arts.html. See also this piece on STEM (science, technology, engineering, mathematics) majors' need for the liberal arts: http://www.usnews.com/opinion/knowledge-bank/2015/05/11/stem-fields-benefit-from-liberal-arts-skills.

[15] William Deresiewicz, *Excellent Sheep: The Miseducation of the American Elite and the Way to a Meaningful Life* (New York: Free Press, 2015), 155.

[16] Martha Nussbaum, *Not for Profit: Why Democracy Needs the Humanities* (Princeton: Princeton University Press, 2010), 2.

CHAPTER 3

THE HEART OF LEARNING

Many who were inspired by the Reformation took their frustrations against an oppressive religious power too far, as in the case of the Peasant Revolt of 1524–25, which Luther and other Reformers condemned. While the Reformers challenged the authority of the papacy, they did not abandon religious authority completely. When power is confronted, opportunities for establishing new authorities often emerge. There were those who, with a rebellious attitude toward religious authority and religion in general, misappropriated the spirit of the Reformation and strayed from traditional orthodoxy, but this is not a strong enough reason to implicate the magisterial Reformers in planting the seeds of modern secularism. What seems common in the contemporary age is that rejecting the power of an institution tends toward the rejection of the basic foundations behind such an institution. More specifically, rebellion against a particular religious order tends to skip past reform and jump straight toward revolution, jettisoning religion *altogether*. This is further complicated by developments in the life of the mind that left religion behind.

In *A Secular Age*, Charles Taylor writes of the transition from a society "in which it was virtually impossible not to believe in God" to one where it was okay—even acceptable—to do so.[1] The burden of proof shifted. Believers today are on the defensive. What happened to faith? Why did faith become a problem of the secular age? An important piece in the development of the modern mind was the rift between faith and reason. The conditions that led to the strain between faith and reason came not during the Reformation, but during the High Middle Ages, when the great theologian and philosopher Thomas Aquinas (1225–1274) articulated a sharp distinction between the limits of reason and the corrective nature of faith. In his attempt to show that faith completed the shortcomings of reason (reason was not totally corrupt, just wounded), Aquinas unintentionally drove a wedge between the two. Reason was not penetrated by faith. Both faith and reason stood separate from one another. Despite efforts to reestablish the supremacy of God's word as it related to salvation but also to reconsider how scripture guided all of life, Protestants continued in this line, failing to recognize the tension between nature (reason) and grace (faith). To be fair, their quest was not a philosophical one, but they assumed a relationship that was philosophically problematic.

The gulf between faith and reason widened with the inauguration of a new scientific method in the early modern period and later with the coming of Enlightenment "reason." Toward the end of the long nineteenth century, faith and religion became a matter not for the public but for the private—not of the rational, but emotional mind. Neither the great Immanuel Kant (1724–1804), who sought to make room for faith in an age of reason, nor revivalism, nor Romanticism, which attempted to situate spirituality in emotion and intuition, could heal the great divorce. And the tension was acutely present at the birth of the modern institution of higher learning. It would behoove me to state more explicitly that the tension between faith and reason, which has remained in the contemporary era, was never inevitable—that is to say, never a problem arising from the natural order of things (i.e., not an ontological problem) but rather directed by an apostate worldview.

By the late nineteenth century, intellectuals were obliged to come to grips with what seemed to be the death of God and of faith. One such individual was Friedrich Nietzsche (1844–1900), a troubled thinker who lived at the height of the secular age. To the ears of conservative evangelicals, the name *Nietzsche* conjures an image of a strikingly intense atheist whose declaration of the death of God—not to mention the death of the once-coveted *über Schnurrbart*—gave birth to a period of epistemic nihilism, political fascism, and total war. But this may be a bit unfair to ole' Fred. Let's put Nietzsche's oft-quoted, but woefully misunderstood comment on the "death of God," in context. The phrase is taken from Nietzsche's Madman in "Parable of the Madman":

> "Whither is God?" he cried; "I will tell you. *We have killed him*—you and I. All of us are his murderers. But how did we do this? How could we drink up the sea? Who gave us the sponges to wipe away the entire horizon? What were we doing when we unchained this earth from its sun? Whither is it moving now? Whither are we moving? Away from all suns? Are we not plunging continually? Backward, sideward, forward, in all directions? Is there still any up or down? Are we not straying as through an infinite nothing? Do

we not feel the breath of empty space? Has it not become colder? Is not night continually closing in on us?
Do we not need to light lanterns in the morning? Do
we hear nothing as yet of the noise of the grave-diggers
who are burying God? Do we smell nothing as yet of
the divine decomposition? Gods, too, decompose. God
is dead. God remains dead. And we have killed him.[2]

The madman's prophetic announcement is really an indict-
ment of the very people who killed God: hubristic enlightened rationalists living in an age when reason dominated,
when man—specifically, "men"—assumed the place of God.
Nietzsche was not informing readers that God suddenly had
a heart attack and died. Rather, the evolution of the modern
intellectual (and political) mind led, if you will, to an evapo-
ration of the knowledge of God. The West no longer needed
God and eventually created the conditions by which it became
increasingly difficult to incorporate God into a new intellectual framework. Modern thinkers either worked to counter
this reality, regardless of their support or opposition, or tried
to find ways to live with it. Nietzsche became one of the latter.
For him, a new morality had to be installed for humanity to
"keep calm and carry on" without God.

Another figure who recognized the reality of an increasingly secular age was the Calvinist polymath Abraham Kuyper
(1837-1920). Like Nietzsche, Kuyper lived at the height of
the modern period, though modernism in Europe began its
long decline with the beginning of the Great War, which had
ended a few years before Kuyper's death. Kuyper's reaction to
secularism was unlike that of North American culture-war
militants of the late-twentieth century. His intent was not
to rollback secularism or reclaim the Christian roots of the
Netherlands. Modernism was here to stay. Rather, Kuyper

engaged secularism in a twofold manner. First, he sought to identify the boundaries where secularism as a religious principle could and could not go in the various social spheres that made up society. Second, he worked to preserve the beliefs and practices of the Christian church. He fought for a confessional church, *"not,"* as he wrote, "a confessional civil society *nor* a confessional state."[3] His liberalism was not directed to counter the secularist, but he would remind the secularist that disbelief should not dictate the goings on of the Christian family, the Christian church, or that of Christian education. (Kuyper was not interested in creating a theonomic state, however. Any effort, Kuyper believed, "to duplicate the situation of Israel, taking Holy Scripture as a complete code of Christian law for the state, would...be the epitome of absurdity."[4]) Kuyper's social outlook rested on the Reformed notion of sovereignty. A consistent view of God's sovereignty seemed to be the best way to keep secularism from becoming total. His great contribution was to interject into the life of the mind the centrality of faith in all of life. Later thinkers in the Reformed tradition would further develop his thought.

Despite the crisis of modern secularism at the end of the most violent period in world history, contemporary academic institutions have been ill-equipped to understand just how to take faith seriously. In my final year in graduate school, I attended a Critical Theory conference. The theme of the gathering was religion in the contemporary academy. Each of the keynote speakers as well as members of the audience agreed that religion could now be incorporated as a legitimate area of study not bound to an older positivist framework. Yet no one agreed on how to do it—how to integrate faith. Part of the difficulty, as I saw it, had to do with the fact that the academy had very little theoretical and practical tools or the imbedded habits to do so. The reintroduction of faith seemed like the awkward reunion of a child with an estranged parent. A revival of a thoroughly Christian liberal arts education may be the first step in mending the relationship between the life of the mind and the life of faith.

Integral Over Integration

Christian institutions have, on at least a theoretical level, maintained a commitment to the integration of faith and learning. "Few themes," writes William Ringenberg, "have received greater emphasis in Christian colleges after 1970 than the integration of faith and learning."[5] *Integration* is a good term when used appropriately. Students are asked daily to analyze (to break apart) and synthesize (put back together), the latter of which relates to integrating (or reintegrating). For V. James Mannoia Jr., "integration presupposes that things not necessarily together are brought together: multiple disciplines, theory and practice, values and learning."[6] In this light, the word is fine. In analyzing water, chemists will distinguish the parts but will never drive a wedge between those components of water and water itself. Such a dichotomy is laughably incoherent.

The question is whether faith is an essential part of learning, of knowing. I believe that it is. The problem with the language of integration, as a larger philosophical issue, is that it gives the impression that faith and learning are by nature separate. Years ago, I watched a professor at a leading Christian university demonstrate in front of a large audience the integrationist approach. His right hand held out faith while his left held out learning. As he slowly brought both hands together, the professor spoke as if his university needed to be the mediator of the assumed tension between the two.

According to Duane Litfin, "Integration is unfortunate. It appears to suggest an exercise in forcing together disparate things."[7] Integration seems to be that awkward—if not unduly time-consuming—task of actively pulling together (and keeping together) two things that need a Supreme Court ruling to wed.

As a healthy working heart is to the body, so faith is to learning. It is never absent. When it comes to this larger question of the relationship between faith and learning, I prefer *integral* over *integration: faith is integral to learning.*[8] What exactly does this mean? Faith is more than a passive guide that accompanies or comes along side learning; rather, it is *the* central engine that drives not just learning but all of life. Faith is a resting and trusting in "something" that brings meaningful coherence to our world, a coherence that is concurrently the source of liberation—of redemption. For Kuyper, faith is "the most fundamental law through which all higher differentiation in our consciousness can come about."[9] We should not take this as so-called blind faith, a faith that lacks certainty. Indeed, the kind of faith described in Scripture is one of confidence of things unseen. If all of life is driven by faith, then there is no learning and no knowledge without faith of some kind (faith in God and His word, faith in reason, faith in the individual mind, faith in the laws of physics, mathematics, or logic, etc.). Faith not only precedes learning but also drives it. Learning without faith is dead.

The Heart

Christian philosophers in the Reformed tradition have used the term *heart* in identifying humanity's faith root, its central drive.[10] Faith moves us to articulate our ultimate concerns, our highest loves, which in turn shapes the dynamic core of our being, the heart. The heart, the "*concentration* and *consumma-tion* of meaning" and being, is both temporal and eternal.[11] That is to say, humans are more than simply flesh and blood. They have been made by God *for* eternity. This, for Herman Dooyeweerd, is the key to our religious nature. Andree Troost explains that "supra-temporality" of the heart "does not mean timelessness, but primarily *being more than temporary,* transcending time":

> Time and all temporal existence find their *fullness* and *con-centration* in the *transcending center:* the human heart.... [The heart] *lives* in time, it *manifests* itself in time; but it is also "more": *as unity and totality* it transcends time (together with all its temporality and diversity). This term also recalls the New Testament idea of the "fullness of time" (or "the times"), an idea which denotes much more than a historical chronological period with certain typical historical situations or "favorable factors."[12]

The heart is the focal point, the holistic meaning-center of all of life, temporal and eternal. How else would anyone be able to know God and His world but through the heart?

Part of what shapes the heart is how we respond to God and His world. All of life has been created, sustained, and given meaning by God the Father through the activity of the second person of the Trinity, the Logos Jesus Christ. God demands from humanity a response to His work, and there are only one of two responses—responses that uncover our basic attitude toward God and directs the entirety of life. According to Romans 1, there are, in essence, only two hearts, two religions in the world. It is through the heart that humans submit to some divine and totalizing Archimedean point upon which everything in the world pivots. "Religion is," Kuyper wrote, "the expression of what is central in our lives. However, degenerate and obscured a people's religion may be, you will always find expressed in it their fundamental ethos. In any given case, this [religious] ethos will be bound up with a people's character and nature, with its history, even with the conditions of the soil on which it lives and the climate in which it breathes."[13] Note that the religious drive is not just individualistic but extends throughout society as a whole. All knowledge claims, nascent thoughts, attitudes, and orientations derive from either a faith reliance on something in the created order, what Dooyeweerd calls *immanence philosophy*, or from the author of such created reality, a transcendent independently self-sufficient being who is sovereign over all, sustains all, and gives meaning to all.[14]

Each part of creation is penultimately dependent on another part. Each of these interdependent parts are, in turn, ultimately dependent on the Creator. The Creator's self-sufficiency and independence makes Him distinct from the creation. This means that no dependent aspect of creation can become independent, for that would make it divine. Let me offer an illustration (at least on the interdependency of the parts of creation). Consider a simple economic transaction between two people. The meaning of the economic is dependent on the social (the two individuals) and the judicial (fair price) life-functions. An economic way of being—just one of many ways of being—is dependent on other ways of being. If one were to assume the independence of the economic, as in the case of an economic determinist, then that aspect—at least ideologically—has been placed in a self-sufficient status, the status reserved only for God. But a dependent aspect of creation *can never* become absolute. All forms of immanence philosophy, whereby the Creator is substituted by creation, are ultimately bound to fail.

If the issues of life flow from the heart, then it is not hard to see that in order to understand life, a major task of a col-

lege education, we must understand the heart.[15] Identifying
the heart enriches our overall understanding of reality. But
the faith-motives behind the development of life are not always explicit. We need to be trained to see. Sharpening critical and creative skills through the liberal arts will allow us to
uncover the ultimate concerns of not only individuals but of
whole societies.

But how do we go about the task of drawing out the heart?
Let's return to the subject of worldview formation. As I mentioned above, worldview formation is a key goal of a liberal
arts education. It also plays a key role in shaping the heart.
The term *worldview* has been used in a number of different
ways. Many understand it as a philosophy of life. It stands
for the way humans interpret the world. But thinkers in the
Reformed tradition understand it differently. Learning begins
with a basic naïve experience, never with a pre-experiential
or pre-articulated theory of it. Indeed, it is the experiences
largely taken for granted that make knowing possible. Our
unique social and cultural situations—our "liturgical habits," to borrow from James K.A. Smith—shape the heart at a
subconscious level. Thus, a worldview begins with experiences we take for granted. It is only afterwards that we find the
words to describe how those earlier experiences have come
to shape our identity. A worldview, therefore, is not a philosophy or a perspective, but is rather something that "yields" a
philosophy.[16] This is why I prefer the term *life-situations* over
that of the often-confusing *worldview*.

Allow me to offer a couple of examples of how life-situations shape the heart. I grew up in a musical household.
My mother is an excellent singer, and my father is an equally
excellent piano player. At a very early age I was introduced to
pop music, show tunes, and of course the classical greats. Music was all around. Although never given formal music lessons,

I began to understand the logic of music in my teen years. I started playing the drums and then moved to guitar; along the way I noticed the patterns inherent to music. When my own children started piano lessons, I did the same, although teaching myself as is my habit. This progression seemed very natural to me, despite the fact that my learning was a matter of catching up. Music's natural feel rested on the fact that it had seeped into my subconscious at a very early age, so I was primed, if you will, for learning. (It might be the case that I have an intrinsic gift for music, but I'm not sure I'd be able to prove that given the undeniable role of my formative extrinsic environment.) The same could be said for those who grow up to be sports nuts. Most likely, the person who develops an intense—sometimes too intense—love for sports, whether for a particular team or just sports in general, often had a parent who inculcated on his or her subconscious mind all things sports related. My nephew, an excellent baseball player, loves the Pittsburgh Pirates. He might try to rationalize such a love as something arising purely from his own interests or because the Pirates are just an incredible team. I doubt it, though. His love for the Pirates—as well as faithfulness to the team—as well as his own athletic capabilities were an inheritance from his father. This in no way means that my love for music or my nephew's love for the Pirates or baseball itself are somehow disingenuous; both loves are very real.

Do these relative circumstances eliminate a shared essence that relate to the heart? Certainly not. But essence is a bit more complicated than we might think. The dynamic heart is closely tied to being, and being is both essence *and* evolution. At first glance, this reads as a contradiction. Let me explain. As in the previous paragraph, my particular love, that which has shaped my heart, is something that has developed over time. Concurrently, I have an essence, a nature, intertwined with my developing heart, serving as the foundation of my status as a religious being. This is the image of God, the unmovable core of being, and my connection with the eternal. Yet I am still shaped by my unique circumstances. The same is true for everyone else. We are, first, image-bearers of God, and we can all think of pivotal moments that have shaped our lives. Such momentous experiences—words of encouragement from a teacher or coach, a traumatic accident, the birth of a child, the death of a loved one, the loss of a job, a moment of profound insight—have transformed our hearts. These influences that come from without are relations that shape the inner heart and provide our deepest meaning.

At the most basic level, our essence as image-bearers of the divine is meaningfully constituted as we stand in relation to the Creator. Humans have been made to commune with God, to respond to Him, to worship and glorify the author of life. But as a result of sin, fallen humanity suppresses such knowledge in unrighteousness and, consequently, begins a new relationship with an idol, the new—and perverted—source of meaning. "In the state of apostasy," writes Dooyeweerd, "the religious impulse, innate in the human heart, turns away from the living God and is directed toward the temporal horizon of human experience with its diversity of modal aspects. This gives rise to the formation of idols originating in the deification of one of these aspects."[17] As mentioned above, we cannot absolutize (make into a self-sufficient entity, for only God contains such an attribute) "what is only relative." The fall does not remove the knowledge of God nor His image. Our epistemic faith-root strengthens the intimate relationship forged with whatever we consider divine. The heart can be changed, however, but not through our rationalizing or emoting. A radical transformation comes through the work of an external agent, the Holy Spirit. The

Spirit redirects our love, beginning on a pre-articulated level, which in turn offers a new life situation. We become aware of our new hearts after the gracious intrusion of the Spirit, who in turn guides us consciously into the light of truth. Every human enters the world within a particular life-situation, a situation that is guided by a faith-motive. As humans mature, they continue to carry that faith-motive, often trying to reconcile one particular drive with other religious drives, multiple faiths. The Christian faith-drive is daily bombarded by competing faith claims.

There is, commendably, an expressed desire to maintain faith and learning in the classroom, but the casting off of one, whether faith or learning (or in some cases both), often occurs when class is over. If all of life is religious, then faith should be behind all of our activities. Sadly, many evangelicals compartmentalize the glue that brings meaning to all of life, or they simply add a spiritual element to their otherwise secular lives. The "value-added" model of Christian education, as Robert Benne calls it, is one where the Christian faith is merely attached to what goes on in the classroom. (Often times it's not attached at all.) According to this model, writes Benne, "Christian teaching and ethos [are] added outside the classroom in faculty-student relationships, revivals, Bible study, worship, and music programs, as well as 'ministry' and social service activities in the larger community."[18] Some schools require a Bible minor to accompany a major that a student might pursue.

This runs counter to the integral faith model advanced in this section. The cordoning off of activities (as in the case of chapel programs) unwittingly deemed more spiritual against those that are not (as in the case, for instance, of a physics class) not only instills a false perception of the space where faith is to be exercised but also adds to the already scandalously anti-intellectualism of the evangelical mind. The worship of God is no less present in an English 101 class than it is in chapel. Princeton's Benjamin Breckinridge Warfield said it best: "Why should you turn from God when you turn to your books, or feel that you must turn from your books in order to turn to God?"[19] Warfield, like many other intellectuals, understood the radical nature of faith in all of life.

Antithesis and Common Grace

Reformational philosophy uses the term *antithesis* to describe the two diametrically opposed beliefs—or, to use Kuyper's language, "world" systems—that inform every aspect of life. In his famous Stone Lectures at Princeton in 1898, Kuyper argued that there needs to be an acknowledgement of "two kinds of human consciousness: that of the regenerate and the unregenerate; and these two cannot be identical":

> [All knowledge] proceeds out of faith. All science presupposes that we ourselves believe; presupposes a belief that the laws of thinking are correct; presupposes beliefs about life; and presupposes above all faith in the principles from which we proceed...the conflict is not between faith and science, but between the claim that the present state of the cosmos is normal or abnormal...it is not faith and science, but two scientific systems that stand, each with their own faith, over against each other...They are both in earnest, disputing with each other across the entire domain of life and cannot desist from the attempt to pull to the ground the entire edifice of each other's contradictory claims.[20]

Kuyper offers something compelling here: When it comes to ultimate moral and cognitively-assenting issues, no common ground exists between Christians and non-Christians. These two opposing viewpoints develop "logically and systematically the whole complex of ruling ideas and conceptions that go to make up our life and world-view."[21] He encouraged Christians to oppose the antithetical worldview of modernism and to "successfully defend" their own sanctuary "by placing in opposition...a life and worldview" of their own.[22] Since Calvinism elevated the sovereign rule as king and "meaning-maker" of all things, Kuyper believed that it offers "the ready solution," the coherent system of philosophical thought, to counter the apostate mind.

Yet the antithesis is not to be understood as a Manichean struggle between the forces of good and evil—an "us versus them" setup—nor should it be confused with the combatants in the "culture wars" that saturates North American political culture. A proper understand of the antithesis, according to Don Petcher and Tim Morris, "does not allow us to simply separate one people against another and be done with it."[23] "We know, after all," Dooyeweerd writes, "that in the heart of the Christian himself the apostate selfhood and the selfhood redirected to God wage a daily warfare...humanity which is renewed in Him still shares in the apostate root of mankind."[24] This is, if anything, humbling vis-à-vis our engagements in life. For those who have been redeemed and justified by grace alone, the antithesis has a twofold meaning. First, it is the Christian's internal battle against the continuing struggle of sin in the life of sanctification. Second, it confronts the external forces set up against God and His work. A renewed mind compels Christians to destroy "speculations and every lofty thing raised up against the knowledge of God."[25]

When talking about the two minds that reveal two oppositional perspectives on the world, Kuyper was not suggesting that the false starting point should be stamped out. As Vincent Bacote reminds us, "Kuyper did not argue that only one group should do science, but that each should be allowed to pursue the discipline in its own circle."[26] Even the idolatrous heart should have the opportunity to explore the world in accordance with its religious principle. A false starting point still abides by the religious order God has implanted in creation. Whatever part (e.g., logic, feeling, aesthetics, biological energy, economics) of creation that the fallen mind takes as the divine center, it remains part of God's good creation and therefore should be preserved. We need to be careful not to throw out the creational baby with the idolatrous bathwater. Dichotomies emerge when believers reject the good creational piece even when it is turned into an idol. Despite its use by the most rabid atheists, logic, for instance, is still highly valued by God. The inclination to declare a part of God's good creation as evil itself is what Reformational philosophers call the "Gnostic tendency."[27] The wheat and the tares, manifested in humanity's most fundamental drive, grow together in these final days. Unfortunately, I think there are times when evangelicals think that the antithesis does not apply to them. While the religious distinction is necessary in separating the redeemed mind from the apostate mind, the line must never become a wall. The antithesis cuts through all of life—even the life of the believer—says Dooyeweerd:

> Many peace-loving Christians have made [the religious antithesis in life and thought] the victim of numerous misunderstandings. They do not recognize that this antithesis does not draw a line of *personal* classification but a line of division according to fundamental principles in the world, a line of division which passes transversely through the existence of every Christian personality. This antithesis is not a human invention, but is a great blessing

from God. By it keeps His fallen creation from perishing. To deny this is to deny Christ and His work in the world.[28]

Discerning the antithesis—the direction of the heart—demands an understanding of its counterpart: common grace. Common grace, or what Calvin referred to as "universal grace," is defined as (1) God's offering of his creation to all of humanity regardless of spiritual state; (2) God's restraining the full devastating consequences of the fall (i.e., bridling the "perversity of nature, that it may not break forth into action," according to Calvin); and (3) the non-elect's ability to have moments of clear insight regarding truth, justice, goodness, and beauty.[29] A familiar passage used to formulate the idea of common grace is Matthew 5:45: "[God] makes his sun rise on the evil and the good, and sends rain on the just and on the unjust." According to Louis Berkof, common grace refers to *"those general blessings, such as rain and sunshine, food and drink, clothing and shelter, which God imparts to all men indiscriminately where and in what measure it seems good to Him."*[30] This is tied to God's sovereignty, for it is He who owns the sun and the rain that are enjoyed by all humans. Humans are offered the freedom to flourish without being immediately judged by God.

Since all humans are image-bearers of God, they have the ability to grasp creational truths. Reason, says Calvin, is "by nature implanted in men...it is certainly a free gift of his beneficence to each...upon pious and impious, it is rightly counted among natural gifts."[31] Although humans are born in sin, "by nature children of wrath, incapable of any saving good," according to the Canons of Dort, they maintain "the glimmerings of natural light," which allows for "some knowledge of God, of natural things, and of the difference between good and evil, and discovers some regard for virtue, good order in society, and for maintaining an orderly external deportment." The "desire to search out the truth," according to Calvin "through natural instinct" is done in order to "foster and preserve society."[32] God has written his law on the hearts of all humans, as Romans 2:14-15 explains: "For when Gentiles, who do not have the law, by nature do what the law requires, they are a law to themselves, even though they do not have the law. They show that the work of the law is written on their hearts, while their conscience also bears witness, and their conflicting thoughts accuse or even excuse them." Scripture provides numerous examples of those outside the covenant of God who without the specific revelation of the law nonetheless exhibit a basic understanding of morality. In his commentary on John 1, Calvin writes, "There is no man, therefore, whom some perception of the eternal *light* does not reach." Calvin's point is further explored along with an appeal to the value of the liberal arts in the opening sections of the *Institutes*:

> You cannot in one glance survey this most vast and beautiful system of the universe, in its wide expanse, without being completely overwhelmed by the boundless force of its brightness. The reason why the author of the Letter to the Hebrews elegantly calls the universe the appearance of things invisible [Heb. 11:3] is that this skillful ordering of the universe is for us a sort of mirror in which we can contemplate God, who is otherwise invisible...*Indeed, men who have either quaffed or even tasted the liberal arts penetrate with their aid far more deeply into the secrets of the divine wisdom.*[33]

Thus, even in the shared cosmos all humans live in communication with the eternal, reinforcing the notion that a liberal arts education is itself a religious endeavor.

In no way does this mean that those without the law are exonerated for their failure to acknowledge the author of such laws. Unbelievers will be condemned for their failure to believe in the saving work of Jesus on the cross; they will equally be condemned for their rejection of God's authorship of creational laws—laws that are *not* the central means of salvation. The antithesis acutely manifests itself when the two world-and-life views engage one common realm in the pursuit of opposing ultimate concerns. The idea of a common realm must not be confused with "neutrality" and should be distinguished from common grace.[34] The antithesis refers to the fundamental orientation of the heart as affected by the fall and redemption; the realm of common grace refers to the creational structures given to Christians and non-Christians alike. Thus, as there is no common ground in terms of *weltanschauung,* there is common ground in how such worldviews are constructed. Christians and non-Christians have the same creational "stuff" from which to work out their basic faith motives. Christians worshipfully affirm the Creator; while non-Christians, although knowing the Creator, suppress Him in unrighteousness. In *Christ and Culture,* Klaas Schilder writes, "Within the framework of time after the Fall, the antithesis was inevitable not in nature but in the use of nature, and hence in culture."[35] Albert Wolter's distinction between structure, "the 'essence' of a creaturely thing," and direction, either the "sinful deviation from that structural ordinance" or the "renewed conformity" in the direction of Christ, is helpful here.[36] The sanctified mind "spreads to the full range of human activities."[37]

A question is often raised that if Christians and non-Christians share in common the works of creation, including the content of their intellectual pursuits, then what difference would the antithesis make in understanding creation? It is true that the heart gives direction to what is common. It is equally true that the antithesis does not change God's truth.

So, again, does it make a difference? We know that the intellectual light, according to Dort, is rendered "wholly polluted" because it is held back "in unrighteousness."[38] There are
some who believe that the unbeliever cannot know anything
truly. I've never been fully convinced of this, for even if unbelievers grab hold of a portion of God's creation in order to
suppress it, they still know that creational element. Are cultural fundamentalists really prepared to say that an unbeliever does not *really* know that 2+2=4? If not, then there is no
reason to enter into a dialogue with the apostate mind. This,
of course, is not an option. But what are we to make of the
"wholly polluted" language used in the Reformed tradition?
Allow me to offer three observations. First, regardless of the
place of the common for all, the unrighteous suppression of
the knowledge of God limits what *could be* a richer appreciation of God's creation. Jason Lief points out that:

> Calvin affirms the role of reason and conscience in the
> temporal realm, while at the same time he expresses
> doubt concerning the ability of reason to know truth
> with any certainty…[Calvin] refers to the 'sluggishness
> of mind',…and says the natural gifts [of reason] have
> been corrupted as the mind is 'plunged into deep dark-
> ness.' Even when he affirms the remnants of 'human un-
> derstanding' that exist after the fall, he goes on to say,
> 'Yet this longing for truth, such as it is, languishes before
> it enters upon its race because it soon falls into vanity.
> Indeed, man's mind, because of its dullness, cannot hold
> to the right path, but wanders through various errors
> and stumbles repeatedly, as if it were groping in dark-
> ness, until it strays away and finally disappears. *Thus, it
> betrays how incapable it is of seeking and finding truth.*'[39]

Second, anyone digging deeper into a particular area of
study will be confronted with anomalies, ironies, or just
plain mysteries that can never be critically and creatively

worked out apart from a theoretical interpretive grid root-
ed in one's religious ground motive. And, again, there are
two basic religious motives. The religious root that rests on
an aspect of creation will be continually frustrated, for it is
impossible to make all things dependent on something that
cannot be independent and self-sufficient itself. Creation
cannot become the Creator. Instead, we must locate the origin and meaning-coherence of creation outside of creation
itself, to a truly self-sufficient non-created being in which all
things depend—namely, the Triune God.

Third, such suppression removes the opportunity to worship the Creator and thus come to a fuller appreciation of the
human condition—an important goal of the liberal arts. As
we'll see in the next chapter, all truth is handed down to us
by an authority. Submission to such authority deepens the
knowledge a student receives. A love for God intensifies the
meaningfulness of what he has given to humanity in creation.

Many evangelicals engage culture for the sole purpose of
battling anything that comes from the unregenerate mind and
therefore refuse to acknowledge the valuable contributions
of unbelievers. These cultural fundamentalists approach the
world with an oppositional attitude. They also value creation
in so far it relates to their own personal salvation. But rejecting the social, economic, aesthetic, and intellectual contributions of unbelievers—even as they come from an idolatrous
root—is to neglect not only a portion of God's creation but
also what he communicates through it. Unbelievers remain
the image of God, which is not only declared good but is also
something that needs to be protected. Richard Mouw suggests that Christians should recognize an element of "mystery
regarding God's dealings with humankind." And we need to
work from "a hermeneutic of caution, though not a hermeneutic of outright suspicion."[40] Unbelievers often do much

better than Christians in battling things like poverty, racism, and sexism. Once again, Mouw encourages believers:

> The same apostle who warns against "all that is in the world" also tells us that "what we will be has not yet been revealed"—that will only be clear to us when 'he is revealed [and] we become like him' (1 John 3:2). Sin still affects the way we think and act. And just as we are not as holy as we might predict on the basis of our theology of depravity. It is a fact of our Christian experience that the church often disappoints us, while the unbelieving world sometimes pleasantly surprises us.[41]

Appreciating the work of those in rebellion to God and his creation takes discernment, humility, and patience. God will complete His work despite the failings of humanity. Even Christians are not ultimately in control of the direction of their transformative cultural activities. Culture is discursive—forces from different directions interact to produce a dynamic phenomenon. An individual who is conscious of what he or she is creating and intending in regard to a potential cultural creation, whether product or habit, may be derailed by external social forces that impose a different meaning and, over-time, a different identity. It is often difficult to trace a neat line from the aim of the doer to its manifestation as a culture. Culture is not only discursive and multidirectional; it is also difficult to control. Culture does not always move from the core to the periphery or from the top down.

In one of his eleven propositions on culture in *To Change The World*, James Davidson Hunter makes the claim that culture is produced in accordance with a "fairly rigid structure" that moves from center to periphery: "The individuals, networks and institutions *most critically involved* in the production of a culture operate in the 'center' where prestige is the highest, not on the periphery, where status is low."[42] Hunter assumes that a traceable line exists between core and periphery (as well as change from the top down as opposed to bottom up). The two are intertwined and mutually constitutive of one another. Today, however, scholars have complicated the relationship between core/periphery and top-down/bottom-up understanding as it relates to cultural production. This should temper the human tendency toward triumphalism. We need to remember that God is the one who ultimately directs not only the heart but culture as well.

The heart is drawn out through a committed engagement to the creational realm that God has given to every member of the human family; such rigorous examinations can be aided by the type of education that this book promotes. A liberal arts education highlights the beauty of our shared creational world and the multiple faith-based perspectives through which meaning is interwoven into the creation. In the end, God's sovereign communication of his Spirit through creation is not dependent finally on the faithfulness of believers, nor completely obliterated by the efforts of unbelievers. Christians are driven by a promise that is now—and will be—fulfilled in the future. All of creation groans under the fall and anticipates renewal. Christians presently live in and engage the world with a newness of mind and heart, anticipating the full reality of the new heavens and new earth. Engaging God's voice through higher education is done in the light of this reality.

Notes

[1] Charles Taylor, *A Secular Age* (Cambridge: Belknap Press, 2007), 3.

[2] Friedrich Nietzsche, *The Gay Science*, Walter Kaufmann, trans. (New York: Vintage Books, 1974), 181-82.

[3] James Bratt, ed., *Abraham Kuyper: A Centennial Readers* (Grand Rapids: Eerdmans, 1998), 197.

[4] Kuyper's quote in James D. Bratt, *Abraham Kuyper: Modern Calvinist, Christian Democrat* (Grand Rapids: Eerdmans, 2013), 142.

[5] William Ringenberg, *The Christian College: A History of Protestant Higher Education in America*, 2nd ed. (Grand Rapids: Baker Academic, 2006), 193.

[6] V. James Mannoia Jr., *Christian Liberal Arts: An Education That Goes Beyond* (Lanham: Rowan and Littlefield, 2000), 126.

[7] Duane Liftin, *Conceiving the Christian College* (Grand Rapids: Eerdmans, 2004), 128.

[8] Although troubled by the language of integration for some time, I was never at a place to offer an alternative term for *integration*. I'm indebted to Robert Sweetman, H. Evan Runner Chair in the History of Philosophy at the Institute for Christian Studies, for helping me find the language to articulate the integral nature of faith learning. See Sweetman, "Christian Scholarship: Two Reformed Perspectives," *Perspectives,* June/July (2001): 14-19.

[9] Kuyper quotation in Ronald A. Kuipers and Janet Catherina Wesselius eds., *Philosophy as Responsibility: A Celebration of Hendrik Hart's Contribution to the Discipline* (Lanham, Maryland: University Press of America, 2002), 32.

[10] Reformational philosophy is a distinctively Calvinistic approach to thinking that can be traced back to the works of Abraham Kuyper (1837-1920) and Herman Dooyeweerd (1894-1977) and Dirk Vollenhoven (1892-1978). These thinkers sought to develop an explicitly Reformed, hence Reformational, way of doing philosophy with a consistent understanding of God's sovereignty as its central motive.

[11]Herman Dooyeweerd, *A New Critique of Theoretical Thought,* vol. 1, "The Necessary Presuppositions of Philosophy," David Freeman and William Young, trans. (Philipsburg: Presbyterian and Reformed Publishing, 1969), 506. Emphasis mine. James Skillen and Rockne McCarthy, ed.., *Political Order and the Plural Structure of Society,* Emory University Studies in Law and Religion (Atlanta: Scholars Press, 1991), 281.

[12]Andree Troost, *What is Reformational Philosophy?: An Introduction to the Cosmonomic Philosophy of Herman Dooyeweerd,* trans. Anthony Runia (Paideia Books, 2012), 177.

[13]Bratt, *Abraham Kuyper,* 198.

[14]Neo-Calvinist and Dooyeweerd scholar, Roy Clouser, author of *The Myth of Religious Neutrality,* has offered a powerful argument defending the idea that all knowledge, even at the basic surface level (e.g., 1 + 1 = 2), reveals foundational religious motives behind them and thus affirms a Christian view of everything. "Is there a Christian View of Everything from Soup to Nuts" *Pro Rege* (June 2003). Clouser makes a distinction between reducibility and irreducibility in the direction of humanity's perspective on the world. The unbelieving mind reduces knowledge to a creation starting point, a foundation derived from a creational thing (e.g., matter for the Marxist). But this is impossible, for matter is dependent on other created things. Thought derived from a Christian root, however, with an irreducible reality, namely, the Triune God, whose being cannot be dependent on anything in the created order.

[15]Proverbs 4:23.

[16]Albert Wolters, "On the Idea of Worldview and Its Relation to Philosophy," in Paul A. Marshall, Sander Griffioen, Richard J. Mouw, eds., *Stained Glass: Worldviews and Social Science* (Lanham: University Press of America, 1989), 14, 24. See Craig Bartholomew and Michael Goheen, *Christian Philosophy: A Systematic and Narrative Introduction* (Grand Rapids: Baker Books, 2013), 18.

[17]Herman Dooyeweerd, *In the Twilight of Western Thought* (Philadelphia: P&R, 1960), 166.

[18]Robert Benne, *Quality with Soul: How Six Colleges and Universities Keep Faith with their Religious Traditions* (Grand Rapids: Eerdmans, 2001), 76.

[19]Warfield quotation in Mark Noll, *Jesus Christ and the Life of the Mind* (Grand Rapids: Eerdmans, 2011), 28.

[20]Abraham Kuyper, *Lectures on Calvinism* (Grand Rapids: Eerdmans, 1931), 131, 133.

[21]Ibid., 137.

[22]Kuyper, *Principles of Sacred Theology*, intro. Benjamin B. Warfield, trans. J. Hendrik De Vries (Grand Rapids: Baker Books 1980), 154, 189-90.

[23]Don Petcher and Tim Morris, *Science and Grace: God's Reign in the Natural Science* (Wheaton: Crossway, 2007), 85.

[24]Dooyweerd, *NC,* 137, 175.

[25]Romans 12:2; 2 Corinthians 10:5.

[26]Vincent Bacote, *The Spirit* in *Public Theology: Appropriating* the *Legacy* of *Abraham Kuyper* (Grand Rapids: Baker Academic, 2005), 82.

[27]Albert Wolters, *Creation Regained: Biblical Basics of a Reformational Worldview,* 2nd ed. (Grand Rapids: Eerdmans, 2005), 61.

[28]Dooyeweerd, *New Critique,* I: III: 1, p. 506.

[29]John Calvin, *Institutes of the Christian Religion,* I:5:3.

[30]Louis Berkhof, *Systematic Theology,* preface by Richard Muller (Grand Rapids: Eerdmans, 1996), 436.

[31]Calvin, *Institutes,* 2:2:14:273.

[32]Ibid., 2:2:13-15.

[33]Ibid., 1:5:1:52. *Emphasis mine.*

[34]Unfortunately, the notion of the antithesis, like most theological extrapolations, may be taken in a multiplicity of directions. In one corner, it has created great confusion; in another, it has created fundamentalist

escapist Christians. At least one Dutch Reformed thinker, Klaas Schilder, challenged the terminology of common grace: "There is indeed 'common' grace in culture (grace for more than one person). But there is no universal (or general) grace for all men. Therefore, Abraham Kuyper's construction was wrong." For Schilder restricting common grace to God's gracious restraint of human depravity, which is generally what theologians mean when talking about common grace, neglects the fact that God also restrains redemption from the non-elect, which cannot be construed as gracious. Theologians define common grace as God's restraining power on fallen humanity and, in some cases, as those moments of true insights that unbelievers can have.

[35]Schilder, *Christ and Culture*, 47.

[36]Wolters, *Creation Regained*, 88.

[37]Ibid., 91.

[38]*Canons of Dort*, Art. IV, in Philip Schaff, ed., *The Creeds of Christendom, With a History and Critical Notes* (Grand Rapids: Baker Books, 1996), 588.

[39]Lief's quote in *Kingdoms Apart*, 233-4.

[40]Richard Mouw, *He Shines in All That's Fair: Culture and Common Grace* (Grand Rapids: Eerdmans, 2002), 93.

[41]Richard Mouw, *Abraham Kuyper: A Short and Personal Introduction* (Grand Rapids: Eerdmans, 2011), 63.

[42]James Davidson Hunter, *To Change the World: The Irony, Tragedy, and Possibility of Christianity in the Late Modern World* (New York and Oxford: Oxford University Press, 2010), 37.

CHAPTER 4

CRITICAL THINKING, CRITICAL WISDOM

Critical thinking is a highly valued skill in the liberal arts. But what exactly does "critical" mean? In one sense, it is the art of reasoning, which centers on logical forms for effective persuasion. Logic is certainly a creational gift from God, ultimately dependent for its particular meaning-function on the Creator. But we often ignore the social conditions and personal disposition—distinct from strict logic forms—that influence rational decisions. This is where wisdom comes into the picture, where the "laws" of rationality intersect with the heart of the rationalist. Reasoning without care or love for others or properly reading a social situation from which a decision must be made can quickly spill over into foolishness.

A Reformed liberal arts education should be concerned with the formation of not only students who can think critically but also wisely. Christians are bound to the notion that true knowledge is inextricably tied to if not interchangeable with biblical wisdom: *to pursue knowledge is to pursue wisdom.*[1] Yet wisdom can be supremely maddening. As far back as I can remember, my father encouraged me to read one chapter from the book of Proverbs every day for an entire month: thirty-one days, thirty-one chapters—not an onerous task even for the most infrequent reader. The habit, with more or less regularity, stuck with me. In the course of studying such penetrating, comforting, and immensely practical words, I found myself frustrated by the paradoxical nature of it all. No matter how diligently we pursue wisdom—even attain it—we can never admit that we "got it." Only fools say such things. An ancient Persian proverb says it well: "A wise man seeks wisdom; a madman thinks he has found it." Wisdom, it seems, is forever elusive and paradoxical.[2] Socrates, one of the wisest thinkers in Western history, referred to wisdom as a "stubborn perversity." It is a fool's quest, but only a fool would ignore the importance of pursuing it—hence, the "stubborn perversity." While far from being wise, my fascination with wisdom has only intensified my desire for it. And Christians cannot escape some element of wisdom any more than they can escape God's gracious work of sanctification.

Thinking wisely does not exactly fit the narrow restrictions of measurability laid out by educational accrediting agencies. Learning outcomes are quantifiable; rarely do they relate to states of being. Wisdom had always been a concern of ancient and medieval philosophy. But with the birth of the modern mind, wisdom, like God, suffered a slow and silent death. Rationality became abstract, separated from the contingencies of social living. The modernist would learn to live without God and wisdom, but this was a profoundly foolish turn. The eventual triumph of reason inaugurated by the father of modern philosophy Rene Descartes (1596-1650), suggests philosopher Richard Rorty in *Philosophy and the Mirror of Nature,* was

> not the triumph of the prideful individual subject freed from scholastic shackles so much as the triumph of the quest for certainty over the quest for wisdom. From that time forward, the way was open for philosophers either to attain the rigor of the mathematician or the mathematical physicist, or to explain the appearance of rigor in these fields, rather than to help people attain peace of mind. Science, rather than living, became philosophy's subject, and epistemology its center.[3]

Champions of the liberal arts need to take seriously Rorty's observation and reconsider wisdom as a learning outcome.

The narrowness of measurability in higher education has also been a marker of what constitutes a valuable student. In an important sense, culture has projected an image of the so-called smart person as a quantifiable object. Wisdom rarely comes into the equation. To be honest, I struggle with the very concept of *smart*. Does smart mean being a STEM major or getting a high score on the SAT? What about the learner whose intellectual awakening fails to abide by the time constraints of contemporary education? Why is the "slow" learner assumed to be and therefore written off as deficient in intelligence? Perhaps I'm not smart enough to offer an answer. From what I've seen, what it means to be a critical thinker or a "smart person" has less to do with figuring out a difficult concept or composing art. Rather, it is about speed. Many students are just not given enough time to learn. Social media has not helped in this regard. Google and that vital organ we call *iPhone* are the brains that think for us. Supposedly "smart" technology fills the crucial spaces left empty by our own ignorance. This is how technology rules over us. The foolish consistency of popular habits makes it very difficult to revive wisdom. Instrumental reasoning, intensified by social media, has worked to uphold the artificial wall between reason and wisdom that had once been erected by human-centered ratio-nalism. Memory, meditation, sustained concentration—these are crucial for developing wisdom. But in our media-driven culture, there is no time. Indeed, capitalism in all its forms has always been the enemy of time. It is not accidental that a market-driven consumer society revels in distractions. Given the frenetic nature of advertising in the information age, dis-tractions are essential to well-functioning consumerism. Sus-tained thought would only get in the way. But contemplation allows us to commune with something, to deepen a love for it as an artist does when stepping back to say "very good" in observation of the beauty of his or her piece.

For Christians, wisdom is *the* foundation of knowing. This chapter highlights a few key aspects of wisdom—au-thority, love, and humility—that should be central in sharp-ening students' critical thinking (and living) skills. The first relates to the willingness to submit to appropriate author-ity. All truth is someone's truth, and following instruction is key to learning that truth. Wisdom is socially embedded; it can be learned by seeing through the outside or through lived experience. We are naturally and subconsciously drawn to—or repelled by—those who can make wise decisions in complicated social situations. We rely on their experience—their wisdom. It's true that we can learn about wisdom from a distance. But we need to be in particular circumstances for a deeper transformative knowing, since wisdom includes living with the consequences of actions in a specific setting. Second, liberal arts learning develops morally concerned cit-izens—citizens who love God and neighbor with both heart and mind. Wisdom is the moral self-evolving from within a social setting. The prudent person knows how to discern social situations, learning from those in similar situations, and make decisions for the welfare of others. Students face an array of challenges, challenges that we submit to in order to eventually become wise. Trevor Curnow understands wisdom as the "ability to cope with whatever life throws at us": "The wise are those who can see the bigger picture, whose horizons are broadest, whose vision is clearest, who live in the light."[4] Finally, there is no learning, no cultivation of love and justice for God and others, without humility. Humility accents our limitations, always reminding us that we are not God. This brings us back to the first feature of wisdom—a reverential submission to the Lord and to others.

Authority

Like faith, authority is essential to learning. This claim, however, is something not easily accepted in our world today. Our hyper-democratic and commercialized culture has put individuals into the long-entrenched habit of rejecting outside instruction. Thinking without the help of others is true knowledge, so we assume. This is a carryover of the eighteenth-century Enlightenment. Kant defined *enlightenment* as man's efforts to free himself from "self-incurred tutelage." Unfortunately, this did not displace the individual mind, but rather exalted it to the highest heavens. Looking at it from a different angle, the Enlightenment did not jettison authority; instead, it merely relocated it. The human mind became the new, absolute authority. And history has shown that idolizing rationalism has had dreadful consequences on the human race.

The foundation and beginning of knowledge/wisdom is a fear, a reverence for God. In this way, it is an active faith, a resting and trusting on *the* ultimate guiding authority. If humans want to live rightly before God, spiritually and physically, they must live in accordance with the order God has put in place in creation. God offers instruction as to how we are to live and, hence, *to be*; He knows infinitely more about His creation than His creatures do, and we obviously learn more about ourselves and the world by heeding His guidance. When seeking knowledge in this way, we must learn, according to Bradley Green, "on His terms." We must think God's thoughts after Him, interpreting and explicating the meaning of creation as He has ordered it. "As creatures," William Dennison writes,

> Our knowledge, like that of the first Adam, is *analogical,* i.e., it is knowledge that is dependent upon the coherence of God's knowledge of Himself and God's knowledge of the creation…Since all facts are determined by and are original with God, humans must freely subordinate their minds to the knowledge of God's knowledge in order to have true knowledge. While for God coherence comes first, for the creature, correspondence has the priority.[5]

Green would agree: It is "incumbent on us to know and understand things in the light of who God is and what He has spoken…We must assent to God's understanding of things if our knowledge is to be in accord with what something really is."[6] The mechanics of coming to know depend on God's sovereignty as manifested in the created order: "We know Him by using the brains He provides. The act of saying we know God uses the vocal chords He has made and the oxygen He supplies."[7] This, of course, carries with it an important moral responsibility on our part. It makes knowledge and morality inextricable: "*All persons know God and are engaged in the moral, willful, ethical submission to or rejection of the God of Holy Scripture at virtually all moments of their existence.*"[8]

Submission to God includes submitting to His creation. First, in order to grow in knowledge and wisdom, humans must submit to His laws embedded in creation. A person who jumps off the roof of a two-story building may strongly believe that he or she will defy gravity. Much to their great embarrassment, however, they will rapidly realize that such an attempt is impossible, given the divine laws of the cosmos, which no human can escape. Included in God's creational order are the human instructors that guide us in knowledge. Wisdom begins with a great respect for God (Prov. 1:7 and 9:10) and His ordered world; that respect follows down to parents, close friends, and teachers. In order to learn the laws of physics, we must submit not only to physical laws embedded in God's world, but also to the physicists—experts who have invested themselves in their chosen field of study—to instruct us. True learners put themselves in the habit of searching out "wise guides," according to philosopher Esther Meek, "We should choose people who are strategically qualified to help us. They expertly know something we need to know in our knowing venture."[9] Everything that we learn has been given to us by an authority—a parent, pastor, thesis advisor, etc. As scientist-turned philosopher Michael Polanyi wrote in *Personal Knowledge*:

> You follow your master because you trust his manner of doing things even when you cannot analyze and account in detail for its effectiveness. By watching the master and emulating his efforts in the presence of his example, the apprentice unconsciously picks up the rules of the art, including those which are not explicitly known to the master himself. These hidden rules can be assimilated only by a person who surrenders himself to that extent uncritically to the imitation of others.[10]

The idea that wisdom comes through wise counselors suggests that it is cultivated from within a community—a community that confirms meaning and confers (perhaps imbues) *us* with meaning. In the case of higher education, communities evaluate the ideas and arguments students advance, not in the sense that the community makes ideas valid—the laws of logic are part of the dynamics of the creational order—but rather approves (or disapproves) of how to use the things inherited from the community. Once again, Polanyi posits, "to accord validity to a science—or to any other of the great domains of the mind is to express a faith which can be upheld only within a community."[11] The shared identity and language of a community, he continues, are the "impulses which shape our vision of the nature of things on which we rely for our mastery of things. No intelligence, however critical or original, can operate outside such a fiduciary framework."[12]

I can remember my elementary school teacher regularly warning us fallow-minded youngsters that truth is never something arrived at by democracy. In one sense, this is correct. The necessarily derived "4" from the propositions "2" and "2" and its mathematical function is not something that is determined by human consensus. 2+2=4 is true no matter who says so. But in another sense—when we move to more sophisticated arguments, arguments made by fallible human beings—"truth" becomes a tad trickier. Professional intellectuals know this full well. It would be foolish for academics to immediately attach undisturbed truth to an argument that they've constructed. The researcher submits a well-constructed argument, lays out a method, and reveals sources. Peers, experts in the same field as the researcher, in turn decide as to whether the scholar has done the appropriate scholarship, whether his or her methods adhere closely with the evidentiary sources. Peer reviewers are less interested in *the* truth as they are in the integrity of the scholarship—and hence the scholar. It is when a community of scholars affirms the work of an individual that "truth," to borrow from William James, "*happens* to an idea."[13] To once again paraphrase Rorty, truth is what our colleagues let us get away with saying. This means that thinkers rely on the authoritative expertise of their peers, who make a judgment as to the soundness of a scholar's work. Higher-level knowledge claims are, from a fallible standpoint, provisional and dependent on others, but such dependency does not eliminate "the possibility of some truths prevailing for centuries, perhaps forever." "[A]ll scientific work has an essentially social character," according to historians Joyce Appleby, Lynn Hunt, and Margaret Jacobs, "The system of peer review, open refereeing, public disputation, replicated experiments, and documented research," they continue, "makes objective knowledge possible. Research programs must be established and findings constantly tested."[14]

An important caveat needs to be made before moving on. When it comes to fallible human authority, we need discernment. Authority can be corrupted. We should not submit blindly or in the absence of wise counselors. There is no reason to accept oppression (though we may have to endure for a time), even when such oppression comes from legitimate authority. Parents, pastors, or government representatives can be abusive. A child is not necessarily acting in a disobedient manner when confronting the violence committed by an abusive parent. Congregants are not in error when confronting the abuses of church leaders. Community organizers are not disrespecting authority by opposing unjust legislation through peaceful means. (What constitutes "injustice" is often a matter of debate, which means it takes wise discernment. I certainly appreciate Martin Luther King, Jr.'s appropriation of St. Augustine and Thomas Aquinas, both of whom believed that unjust laws are no laws at all and therefore need not be obeyed.) We can find many other examples.

Love

How do we distinguish God-honoring from God-dishonoring authorities? How do we distinguish wisdom from foolishness? We can say that one who commits an immoral act is a fool. Yet the identity of a fool is not always tied to an immoral act. A fool can objectively do the right thing, but nonetheless remain a fool. The fool is one who depletes the potential flourishing of the person or persons they interact with. The opposite is true when it comes to wisdom. A wise individual exhibits a proactive morality—a morality that takes joy in cultivating the well-being of others. We often restrict morality to prohibitions. But a wise act not only includes a prohibition against, say, murder, but a proactive action that betters the life of the individuals affected by a wise decision. Not only does a wise person humbly submit to instruction, adding years to his or her life, but he or she also adds to the life of others. In short, wisdom fosters love for others.

In *The Idea of a Christian College: A Reexamined for Today's University,* authors Todd Ream and Perry Glanzer suggest that the goal of a Christian institution of higher learning "involves teaching students how to love God with their whole being (their heart, soul, mind, and strength) and to do so in multiple contexts (as a student, neighbor, citizen, friend, etc.)."[15] The goal of a liberal arts education should be toward the flourishing of creation. Ream and Glanzer continue:

> If one thinks about the creation of music or the creation of learning about engineering, architecture, or chemistry, it is easy to think about the productive discussions and directions such conversations might take. For example, consider the question: How can an architect creatively design a home or a civil engineer creatively

construct a highway system so that it maximizes human flourishing and stewardship of God's creation?[16]

For philosopher Nicholas Wolterstorff, the end of education is to instill within students a desire to "dwell" in shalom—"to find delight in living rightly before God, to find delight in living rightly in one's physical surroundings, to find delight in living rightly with one's fellow human beings, to find delight even in living rightly with oneself."[17] Students should bring shalom by attending to the "moral wounds" of the fallen world.[18] As agents of reconciliation, Christians are to bring the light of the gospel to a fallen world through the verbal proclamation of the word and the fruits of being made right before God—i.e., good works. Students should have an interest in returning the world to a right or just relationship to God. We should not think that this type of justice is one in which Christians redeem in a saving sense the things in the world, though Christians are engaged in redeeming activities—i.e., activities that come from a transformed life.

Concern for God and neighbor instilled within us through wisdom reformats the way we understand morality. Morality reveals itself as we interact with others. Educator Howard Gardner argues that the concept of a moral good—what he refers to as "neighborly morality"—constitutes "a property of our relations with other human beings—including whom we know well and also those who are unfamiliar; groups, both close and remote; and, less directly though equally important, individuals with whom we have relations as a result of our work or our membership in a profession."[19] Morality depends partly on how we see others treated. For Patricia Churchland, the interlocking brain processes connected to morality are sharpened in and through our social behavior in a number of ways:

> (1) *caring* (rooted in attachment to kin and kith and care for their well-being), (2) *recognition of others' psychological states* (rooted in the benefits of predicting the behavior of others), (3) *problem-solving in a social context* (e.g., how we should distribute scarce goods, settle land disputes; how we should punish the miscreants), and (4) *learning social practices* (by positive and negative reinforcement, by imitation, by trial and error, by various kinds of conditioning and analogy).[20]

Our loves, desires, and passions are fostered by how we perceive and interact with others' loves, desires, and passions. As mentioned already, much of what we come to love and enjoy as adults stems from a parental love passed down. Like the heart and being that constitutes the self, the development of morality depends on social context. "At the root of moral practices," Churchland continues, "are social desires; most fundamentally, these involve attachment to family members, care for friends, the need to belong."[21]

This type of morality encourages us to read properly social circumstances. We're often reminded not to answer a fool according to his or her folly. But we rarely meditate on the times when we *should* answer a fool. It is incumbent on a person to discern the situation that would lead to making a decision one way or the other. The way we speak or how we position our gaze—apart from the verity of our claims—can be manifestations of either wisdom (Prov. 17:24) or foolishness (Prov. 12:16). Learning how to become wise or foolish requires looking in on or being a part of a social context that would show us the differences. The wise person takes time to evaluate the setting and weigh the impact of a potential action, considering the positive results of an action. A fool takes the easy route: opens his or her mouth wide, fails to listen, and disregards how others feel. The wise person chooses the more difficult path: closes the mouth, listens intently, and cares deeply for others. The social goal of the fool is the elevation of the self. The intent of the wise is the peace and well-being of the community.

In pursuing the good of others, we must selflessly concern ourselves with others, but this does not entail trumping our individuality in the process of becoming members of a group.[22] Losing ourselves beyond proper submission holds significantly negative consequences. Humans have a tendency to "deindividuate" themselves when they conform to a group. Acceptance is a fundamental human desire. Numerous studies have demonstrated the tendency to become someone—a sadistic torturer in the Stanford case, or a willing executioner in the Milgram experiment of the early 1960s—who we would be opposed to otherwise. This kind of negative "deindividuating" is not something supported by wisdom. Wisdom preserves the individual through opening up to the other, doing so for the good of both.

Whatever action we finally take after reading a situation, we must begin and end with love. True love for others requires our whole being—knowledge of what "is" right and wrong and a loving concern for how doing something (right or wrong) may affect someone. Wisdom, then, is a combination of both critical reasoning and emotional investment. Separating reason and emotion—and I acknowledge both terms are bigger than the way I'm using them—brings us further away from making wise decisions. The Hebrew word for wisdom, *hokmah,* refers to "both the mind *and* the heart," in the words of Stephen Hall. Reason and emotion are inextricably linked. Heart and mind, reason and emotion are not "distinct parts, mind you, but marbled together."[23] Every decision, which can be found in the "the medial prefrontal cortex and perhaps the ventral striatum," requires the two.[24]

In his best-selling book *Descartes' Error,* for instance, Antonio Damasio has argued that severe damage to the prefrontal cortex detaches the emotional element that is indispensable for reason and by consequence sociability. In *Orthodoxy,* G. K. Chesterton writes: "The madman is not the man who has lost his reason. The madman is the man who has lost everything except his reason."[25]

Proverbs demonstrate that true knowledge includes both reason and emotion. Making a reasonable decision requires emotional regulation. We should avoid fools who speak loudly without thinking (Prov. 17:28; 18:17). Speaking without appropriate reasoning is the ruin of fools (Prov. 13:3). Likewise, the fool is the one who cannot control his temper; he does not exhibit emotional control (Prov. 14:29; 16:32; 19:17; 22:24). Control of the temper is better than the conquest of a city (Prov. 16:23). From the understanding that decisions are made with both reason and emotion, we can affirm that wisdom is holistic, "a mystery which resists partitioning," writes Edward Farley.[26]

Love for others embraces empathy, the ability to imagine another's situation.[27] *Empathy* means to willfully step "outside the moat of one's own self-interest to understand the point of view of another."[28] It's true that the fall has made us self-centered creatures, but humans at the same time are hard-wired to imagine the conditions of others. Adam Smith referred to this "antithesis of selfishness" as the "impartial spectator"; the famous social reformer Jane Adams called it "affectionate interpretation[s]." Imagining one's self in the place of another, according to Brian Schwartz and Kenneth Sharpe, "reflects the integration of thinking and feeling," referring back to *hokmah.*[29] Prior to the discovery of mirror neurons was the simulation theory, "whereby," writes Gazzaniga, "we put ourselves in another person's shoes and figure out what we'd do in his or her situation."[30] "This tendency," he continues, "to react to the distress of others appears to be innate: it has been demonstrated in newborn infants, who cry in response to the distress of other infants within the first days of life."[31] The neurons that generate empathy also produce a sense of altruism, activated by the insular cortex, which makes us value other people. The proactive morality that one finds in empathy and altruism is guided toward equity, justice, and overall goodwill beyond the self. The brain, in other words, is made to feel and understand the sufferings of other beings; wisdom, in turn, allows us to find ways to alleviate such sufferings. But balance is key. Too much empathy, it must be noted, may cause someone to make a poor decision. In empathizing with someone who struggles with an addiction, for instance, we must understand their condition, yet at the same time we must be disinterested, in an objective sense, to aid in recovery. Seeing a loved one in such great pain may get in the way of treatment, since there is a tendency to over empathize. We may not know how to give aid. We may also become unwitting enablers that further the sickness. What we need to do is quietly come alongside the one in need, to empathize for the purpose of moving toward healing.

Humility

Existentialist philosopher Jean-Paul Sartre once wrote that "man is fundamentally the desire to be God."[32] There is certainly a ring of truth in this. The fool's intransigence toward God stems from a jealous desire *to be* God, which tends toward a lofty view of self. An absolute necessity for wisdom is an attitude of humility (Proverbs 11:2). A key element of humility is the recognition of our limitations, which refers not only to what we know (or think we know), hence the reliance on wise counselors, but also how we deal with the unknown. The human-centered "enlightened" mind has been incapable of dealing with the unfamiliar, pursuing certainty with an attitude of infallibility. Rarely are we given answers to major issues we face in life. Eliminating "uncertainty," writes William Deresiewicz, "eliminates life."[33] The demand for immediate answers may not lead to the elimination of life, but it certainly makes it quite dull. The details of our lives are not laid out before us, and rarely are we given answers to the major issues we face. Knowing how to live does not rest on having our entire lives laid out before us. Learning *how* to live requires accepting the unknown. This is patience, which itself presupposes humility, a necessary condition for wisdom.

While we have the social components (communities) and cognitive faculties necessary for wisdom (reason and emotion), it is "not automatic," according to Brian Schwartz and Kenneth Sharpe. Wisdom "must be nurtured by experience."[34] All experiences "will have elements in common with past situations, which is what enables us to profit from past experiences." They continue, "The patterns we learn come largely from feedback—trial and error."[35] Gene Fant writes, "Wisdom is the ability to know what to do in a given situation and the courage to actually do it." Experience allows us to withdraw "knowledge from the bank of information" in order to "address the world's challenges."[36] The wise "store up knowledge" as Proverbs 10:14 states. Individuals become wise because they've grown from experience, hence the honor bestowed on the "hoary head" (Prov. 16:31). Wisdom comes with age, and the experiences that prepare us for its reception usually coming in degrees of adversity. This is the nature of social learning. We can see this in young children, who are not always in control of their emotions as they begin the process of interacting with other people in different contexts. Emotional stress is often caused by the inability to interpret and find stability in new experiences. Generally speaking, younger people tend toward frequent emotional outbursts, while older people are able to stabilize emotions and find explanations for a more positive outlook. The emotionally stable individual has a better grasp of the world, because they've had more time to live in it.

The more we draw from our experiences, especially ones that present a moral issue for us to settle on, the more emboldened we are to offer solutions. Having a storehouse of experiences, older and hopefully wiser people better understand the nature of the world and are more equipped to handle new realities over the long term. (Let's not be naïve, however. Certain crises are much more difficult to overcome. An altercation on the playground among toddlers is a less intense form of adversity in the evolution of our personality than, say, the impact of sexual or physical abuse on a young child. Hall affirms this: "Early stresses in human life can trigger a textbook's worth of human pathology; resilience is a puzzle precisely because some people gain strength from these early challenges."[37]) Humility moves us, Hall writes, "to a higher level of understanding, almost intuition, of knowing when experience should guide decisions and when you have to throw out the experiential playbook and literally do a rethink."[38] Young people need to learn how to "cope with enigma and adversity, tear down strongholds, and thus to promote the life of an individual and/or community."[39]

Accepting the unknown should not give us an excuse to live irresponsibly. When deciding on a spouse, starting a family, switching jobs, or choosing a college—do we really know what to expect within those experiences? This should not lead us to an irresponsible life. We can make sure whether or not we are financially ready, have the appropriate test scores, or demonstrate the proper professional skills, but we'll never know what life will bring to us in any situation. Success requires listening to the instruction of others (wise parents, fellow employees, or school counselors) and learning from experience—from the unknown. Mistakes *will* be made; fools refuse to acknowledge this irrefutable truth. We accept the reality that there will always be new experiences in order to learn how to live.

The reader may have noticed up to this point the emphasis placed on the individual's cultivating an attitude of humility from within. But humility can also be forced upon us from without. We often have no choice but to submit to our humbling circumstances. This is a reality for those who face overwhelming opposition for the sake of truth. Picturing a wise person may conjure images of a taciturn Jedi-warrior ready to cut us down with a single word or a swift deadly strike, but some of the most celebrated sages in history—Socrates, Jesus, and Martin Luther King, Jr., to name a few—were not properly honored in their own time. They were murdered. The altruistic and compassionate person, concerned for the long-term well-being of others, is often the lone representative of truth and justice; they willingly give their lives confronting ignorance and pride. Living in such great adversity, in the shadow of death, forces the wise to identify, choose, and attend to the things that are important in life. Death "sharpens our eyes for details about the well-lived life and whets the edges of our hearts and minds as we cleave to decisions and behaviors that aspire to be wise."[40] But living emotionally stable lives in the face of death should not lead to hedonistic nihilism, existential angst, or some kind of Platonic escapism. Instead, wisdom should generate a desire to find ways of making life better even for those opposed to the voice of wisdom. In this way, wisdom will always move toward reconciliation—toward redemption.

If wisdom is cultivated in the unknown, then it would be good for students to be trained liberally, so that they might be better equipped to engage a host of experiences. They may not be equipped to tackle everything that comes their way, but they'll certainly have the emotional stability to work through such challenges. According to Meek, knowing—more importantly the process of coming to know—is both a pilgrimage and a gift whereby the knower commits or pledges in faith to what is yet to be known. This journey begins with wonder, with an adumbrated love—a love of the journey itself—not yet fully articulated. "The knowing venture," Meek continues, "calls us to trust ourselves to something we seek to know, to trust ourselves to its developments, to trust ourselves to a reality that is relationally responsive and generous, to trust ourselves to relationship, to trust ourselves to carefully chosen guides and to companions on the journey, to trust ourselves in the knowing venture."[41] The liberal arts provide the skills for students to cope with the unknown. College, writes Anthony Kronman, "is not just a place for the transmission of knowledge but a forum for the exploration of life's mystery and meaning through the careful but critical reading of the great works of literary and philosophical imagination that we have inherited from the past."[42] College students enter dialogue with the works of great thinkers, appropriating the ideas and practices—i.e., the experiences—in the history of human thought to their own circumstances. Learning how to live in the unknown should encourage us to consume (in large doses) a variety of subjects, augment the great cloud of wise counselors (authors) that already surround us, and invest in a host of experiences.

The fear (reverence and awe that leads to submission) of the Lord is the beginning of wisdom, knowledge, and, ultimately, life. God's wisdom is a humbling sword, since it exposes our hearts (and the hearts of others), shatters our foolish pride, and forces us, with the power of the Holy Spirit, to move outside the self to our transcendent-immanent Creator. True knowledge—a whole-person love of God—reveals what we owe to the One who owns everything. As sinners, we foolishly suppress the knowledge of the invisible God and exchange it for an image of our own making. Only God's grace—an alien or unknown grace coming to us from without—can truly humble us. When we submit to Him in reverence and awe, we enter the most important social relationship, a covenantal relationship. This is the beginning of true wisdom—a stubborn perversity, perhaps, but one that reveals the magnificence of our stubbornly loving God.

Notes

[1]I'm not suggesting that educators are incapable of providing a rubric to assess wisdom. Perhaps the following markers could be included in measurable outcomes: identifying student involvement in community activities, considering how they deal with stress, evaluating their attitude toward professors, administrators, and staff members. A campus alumni coordinator might also keep in contact with alumni to see how their current lives—church membership, family status, and vocational activities—reflect the goals of practical wisdom.

[2]For Elkhonon Goldberg the wisdom paradox is that while our cognitive faculties may become worn or less sharp with age our life-experiences augment, helping us become wiser. See Elkhonon Goldberg, *The Wisdom Paradox: How Your Mind Can Grow Stronger as Your Brian Grows Older* (London: Simon & Schuster, 2005). See also Trevor Curnow, *Wisdom: A History* (London: Reaktion Books, 2015).

[3]Richard Rorty, *Philosophy and the Mirror of Nature* (Princeton: Princeton University Press, 1981), 61.

[4]Trevor Curnow, *Wisdom: A History* (London: Reaktion Books, 2015), 9, 10.

[5]William D. Dennison, *A Christian Approach to Interdisciplinary Studies: In Search of a Method and Starting Point* (Eugene: Wipf and Stock, 2007), 88.

[6]Bradley G. Green, *The Gospel and the Mind: Recovering and Shaping the Intellectual Life* (Wheaton: Crossway, 2010), 163.

[7]Ibid., 161.

[8]Ibid., 162.

[9]Esther Meek, *A Little Manual for Knowing* (Eugene: Cascade Books, 2014), 42.

[10]Michael Polanyi, *Personal Knowledge: Towards a Post-Critical Philosophy* (Chicago: University of Chicago Press, 1974), 53.

[11]Michael Polanyi, *Science, Faith, and Society: A Searching Examina-*

tion of the Meaning and Nature of Scientific Inquiry (Chicago: University of Chicago Press, 1964), 73.

[12] Michael Polanyi, *Personal Knowledge: Toward a Post-Critical Philosophy* (Chicago: University of Chicago Press, 1962), 266.

[13] Louis Menand, ed., *Pragmatism: A Reader* (New York: Vintage Books, 1997), 114.

[14] Joyce Appleby, Lynn Hunt, and Margaret Jacobs, *Telling the Truth About History* (New York: W.W. Norton, 1989), 458, 461.

[15] Todd C. Ream and Perry L. Glanzer, *The Idea of a Christian College: A Reexamintation for Today's University* (Eugene: Cascade Books, 2013), 4.

[16] Ibid., 55.

[17] Nicholas Wolterstorff, *Educating for Shalom: Essays on Christian Higher Education,* Clarence W. Joldersma and Gloria Goris Stronks, eds. (Grand Rapids: Eerdmans, 2004), 23.

[18] Ibid., 24.

[19] Howard Gardner, *Truth, Beauty, and Goodness Reframed: Educating for the Virtues in the Twenty-First Century* (New York: Basic Books, 2011), 78-79.

[20] Patricia Churchland, *Braintrust* (Princeton: Princeton University Press, 2012), 8.

[21] Ibid., 12.

[22] Bruce Hood, *The Self-Illusion: How the Social Brain Creates Identity* (New York and Oxford: Oxford University Press, 2013), 118.

[23] Stephen Hall, *Wisdom: From Philosophy to Neuroscience* (New York: Knopf/Doubleday, 2010), 45.

[24] Ibid.

[25] G.K. Chesterton, *Orthodoxy* (Rockville: Serenity Publishing, 2009), 17.

[26]Farley quote in Hodgson, *God's Wisdom*, 89.

[27]Hall, *Wisdom*, 142.

[28]Ibid., 116.

[29]Brian Schwartz and Kenneth Sharpe, *Practical Wisdom: The Right Way to Do the Right Thing* (New York: Penguin Books, 2010), 71.

[30]Gazzanaga, *The Ethical Brain*, 173.

[31]Ibid., 175.

[32]Jean-Paul Sartre, *Existentialism and Human Emotions* (New York: Citadel Press, 1995), 63.

[33]William Deresiewicz, *Excellent Sheep*, 111.

[34]Schwartz, *Practical Wisdom*, 68.

[35]Ibid., 102, 105.

[36]Gene Fant, *The Liberal Arts: A Student's Guide* (Wheaton: Crossway, 2012), 52.

[37]Hall, *Wisdom*, 222.

[38]Ibid., 193.

[39]Waltke quote in Robert Saucy, *Minding the Heart: The Way of Spiritual Transformation* (Grand Rapids: Kregel, 2013), 195.

[40]Ibid., 270.

[41]Meek, *Little Manual*, 29.

[42]Anthony Kronman, *Education's End: Why Our Colleges and Universities Have Given Up on the Meaning of Life* (New Haven: Yale University Press, 2007), 6.

CHAPTER 5

COMMUNAL SELF, COMMUNAL LEARNING

According to a Higher Education Roundtable study sponsored by Pew Charitable Trust in the mid-1990s, "The liberal arts college embodies the ideal of learning as an act of community."[1] A liberal arts education is a journey of self-discovery. Students come to find, even help create, who they will become. And in the *Christian* liberal arts setting, as we've seen in previous chapters, young adults come to understand who they are as image bearers of God. From first year to senior year, every experience, whether in or out of the classroom, should be one in which students ask their fundamental teleological question: "How, in this situation, can I learn to glorify God and enjoy Him?" The answers are central to self-discovery and self-fulfillment in Christ, the source of our true self. And the journey of self-discovery requires others. A Christian college provides a place to commune with God and other humans and thereby cultivate a deep sense of self. According to educator Parker Palmer,

> The whole culture of the academic community…works
> to shape our views of self and world. In fact, the rules
> and relationships of a school comprise a "hidden cur-
> riculum" which can have greater formative power over
> the lives of learners than the curriculum advertised in
> the catalogue. A business school may offer courses in
> team management and collective work styles, but if the
> culture of that school requires students to survive those
> courses through competition, then competition and not
> cooperation is the real lesson taught and learned. In a
> thousand ways, the relationships of the academic com-
> munity form the hearts and minds of students, shap-
> ing their sense of self and their relation to the world.[2]

"A community, be it family or church or college," Arthur
Holmes concludes in his now classic work, *The Idea of a Christian College,* "is perhaps the single most powerful influence in
shaping a person's values. It is therefore of major importance
that [college educators] shape that community well."[3]

A Christian liberal arts institution communicates the spirit
through community.

The Communal Self

The modern mind tends to divorce the individual from his
or her social environment. We find ourselves surrounded by
advertisements about going our own way, not following the
crowd, being a stand-alone visionary or trailblazing entre-
preneur. Nothing but our will determines who we are. This
might sound empowering, but it's altogether delusional. Modern culture has made an idolatrous "ism" out of the individual.
The idea of being totally alone would instill terror in the heart
of the most courageous existentialist. When thinking about
what it would be like to be truly alone, I'm drawn to that line
in the Apostle's Creed about Christ's descent into hell. What

exactly does it mean? I agree with those who say that the phrase refers to Christ's suffering in life and in death, especially His agonizing experience of facing the full wrath of God the Father. Consider how the wrath of the Father upon the Son was also a moment of true loneliness.[4] I suspect that many believers fear hell because it is the place of extreme temperatures and insatiable annelids. But should we not be more terrified of being abandoned by God? I often think that Christ's hell was the state that God did not intend for humanity and certainly not for the Godhead—namely, to be truly alone, rejected by both God and humans. The absence of God from our perspective on the world troubles us at a deep level. Yet despite fallen humanity's dogged efforts to suppress the creator of the universe, living life with an accusing conscience, the creator is never really gone. As the Psalmist asks, where is it possible to hide from God? The attempt of fallen humanity to separate from God is the epitome of foolishness (Ps. 14:1). Absolute isolation from the divine would be a reality beyond our worst nightmare.

We would have a similar—but admittedly nowhere near as horrific—experience if we were isolated from other humans or from a healthy environment. Humans can never exist alone—neither apart from God nor fellow beings. Both self and world are bound together, mutually constituted in a holistic union. I mean this not in the sense that other people and our particular social environments simply influence who we become. This idea assumes that a universal or transcendent "I" or ego exists separate from externalities; rather, both self and environment, dynamic processes stabilized by divine law, play a central role in creating the individual self. We can illustrate this process of becoming by returning to the brain, an essential part of selfhood that is "powerfully shaped" by its environment, argues psychologist Curt Thompson, "No one's mind functions completely independently from the minds of others. There is no such thing as a self-made man or woman."[5] This must be taken seriously. It would be hell to be totally abandoned, without others and without God. Identity is interwoven and dependent on creative adaptations to particular social and cultural environments put in process, upheld, and ultimately determined by God the creator.[6] The formation of community and the meaning that comes from it would not be possible without functioning, interconnected minds in dialogue. Personhood, what constitutes our unique individuality, rests on the working of the mind and the community from which it comes.

By community, I mean a live community of learners together. An artificial world creates an artificial self. Compared to a traditional classroom, a virtual community falls short of effective learning. I'll admit that there is something mysterious about interacting with an instructor and fellow students that amplifies the learning experience. The creation of massive open online courses (MOOCs) has augmented the opportunity to continue one's education. Early zealots of this mode of education thought that it would revolutionize learning, displacing traditional methods. But traditions, like habits, die hard. Studies have shown that a large majority of individuals taking such courses prefer traditional face-to-face classroom interaction.[7] What is more, persistency rates for these classes are deplorable, some as low as 4%.[8] And those who have rushed in to establish online programs have failed to discover gold in them thar hills.

The online market has been monopolized by a few educational giants. Don't get me wrong, there is certainly a place for online education, especially for professional adults who want to take an exciting course here or there. An individual can certainly gain knowledge this way, but at this level the learning corresponds with the maturity of the learner—a maturity achieved through the process of mimicry. As of yet the evidence for the effectiveness of MOOCs over that of traditional learning—even when programs simulate live, face-to-face teaching—has been found wanting.[9] MOOCs feed our desire not for independent thinking but isolationism (escapism), intensifying the *togetherness-separation* and *escapist-enslaving* paradoxes. Susan Pinker, author of *The Village Effect,* argues that face-to-face interaction, instead of mediated social interaction through communication technology, remains the prime contributor to a longer, healthier, and even successful life.

Scientists have been able to relate cognitive development with the natural instinct for social interaction. An animal's social behavior varies with the size of the brain. Bigger brains, especially the human brain, according to Bruce Hood, "facilitate social behavior."[10] The brain of a locust, for instance, enlarges by 1/3 when it enters a swarm. Some primates like chimpanzees are more social than gorillas; the cortex of the former is more developed and larger than the latter. Damage to the brain as a result of early social neglect—and this includes increased hours of "screen time"—shrinks the brain in terms of what could be its fuller development and has resulted in a severe deficiency in emotional regulation, decision making, and social connectivity.

One way to better understand the constructive role of the environment in our social, cultural, and cognitive development is to reflect on the familiar nature-nurture debate. Our nature and our nurturing environment go hand in hand. It's nearly impossible to draw a line separating the two. Exposure to repeated social habits, positive or negative, shapes basic personality. "Genes are the scaffolding," Michael Gazzaniga believes, "but the fine detail is fine-tuned by interaction with the environment; a pure genetic description of the human species does not describe a human being."[11] In *Cognitive Science, Religion, and Theology: From Human Minds to Divine Minds,* author Justin L. Barrett writes that "no aspect of our biological development, let alone our cognitive development occurs without important contributions from both our biological endowment and our environment":

> Cells don't divide and multiply without a steady stream of chemical nourishment from their environment, pre-natal development is dependent upon hormones and nutrients from the mother, and babies simply cannot survive, let alone develop properly, without massive environmental inputs. When it comes to human thought and behavior, we see more of the same. If eyes do not receive stimulation from the environment, our ability to see properly is compromised, but without eyes and the visual cortex, we won't see properly either. Learning a language requires exposure to that language but also requires the right biological substrate. You cannot teach a rabbit German because it does not have the right biological substrate. For any cognitive capacity of any behavior you come up with, the answer to "Is it nature or nurture?" is always "Both," and deciding if it is more one than the other may prove impossible because "nature" and "nurture" are so vague.[12]

If God has made humans as social and communal beings, experiencing considerable pain when separated from others (e.g., long-term social isolation), then we must acknowledge a social world beyond the individual self, a world that shapes us in a more holistic manner.

Mirroring Others

UCLA behavioral scientist Matthew Lieberman makes the case that cognitive development is a matter of multiple brains interacting with one another. The brain, he writes in *Social: Why Our Brains Are Wired to Connect,* not only depends on other brains for its development but is structured in such way that it *cannot help but to think about and empathize with the minds of others.* This consists of the ability to sense how others are feeling or thinking. Self and social environment form an interwoven piece. Practically speaking, "self" is formed through constant mimicking and empathizing. We become who we are by imagining ourselves as someone else and then acting on that imagination. To say it differently, the habits of others provide models for our own self-creation, becoming who we are by actively pursuing who we are not. "[O]ur brains are hardwired to resonate with other brains," according to Richard Restak, "whenever we observe another person's behavior, a mental representation of that behavior occurs in our own brains."[13]

Learners, at any stage of development, move through the unknown (ignorance) to knowing by faithfully attending to the authority of another. Kids mimic the behavior of their parents. These imitation routines are unconsciously inculcated on the minds of young children, shaping their orientation. And they continue to mirror the actions of others—whether teachers, peers, celebrities, etc.—as they get older and develop a sense of their own independence. This is all part of a socio-cognitive loop. "[O]ur thoughts and behaviors," Restak says, "are powerfully influenced by other people's actions...As you observe my hand reaching for the cup, the motor cortex in your brain will also become slightly active in the same areas you would use if you reached out to pick up that teacup. Further, if you watch my lips as I savor the tea, the area of your brain corresponding to lip movements will activate as well."[14]

The social apparatus of the larger human brain is demonstrated not simply in the desire to commune with others, but also to conform. "Our need to conform is a powerful force that shapes us and literally changes the way we think. In other words, it is not just public compliance when we conform to the group but true private acceptance of group norms."[15] It is quite astounding how individuals can be swept up by the actions of others. We objectively distance ourselves from the deplorable actions of an unruly mob that we might see on television, for instance, but the experience is much different when we are in one. Peer pressure is not something from which humans eventually graduate. (I can already hear the naysayers: "Oh, no. I'm not influenced by anyone. I'm in control of my own mind." Unique like everyone else, right? In my years of teaching, I've noticed that the younger the student the stronger the naysayer and more committed conformist.)

Most people think that they are mental stalwarts when it comes to being swallowed up by a crowd, but studies conflict with such a position. According to Hood, "Other people trigger our emotions reflexively. As soon as we are in a crowd we become aroused. The limbic system that controls our behavior responds automatically to the presence of others. Arguably, this is the basic function of emotions—to motivate social behavior to either join or avoid others."[16] As mentioned in the previous chapter, the move to be part of the group is referred to as "deindividuation." This is not so much our tendency to reject or forfeit our individual agency, but rather, when emotions are stimulated within the limbic system because of the actions of others, we tend to "trump" our individuality for the sake of the group. Conformity, then, seems to be a natural part of the human condition.

The ability to mimic and thereby show our connection to others has been redoubled by the relatively recent discover of the brain's mirror neurons. Like most groundbreaking discoveries in science, the discovery of these particular neurons happened by accident. Using macaque monkeys, a team of neurophysiologists led by Giacomo Rizzolatti had been studying the "part of the neocortex concerned with planning, selecting, and executing actions."[17] They focused on the grasping triggers or motor cells in the brain. One day a member of Rizzolatti's team reached for something and instantly "heard a burst of activity from the computer that was connected to the electrodes that had been surgically implanted in the monkey's brain." The monkey had not been grasping for anything. It sat there motionless. The neurons had been activated simply by watching the scientist grasp for something. This unplanned moment was later initiated by another team member who picked up a peanut, which in turn activated the mirror neurons once again. UCLA's Marco Iacoboni writes, "Cells in the monkey brain that send signals to other cells that are automatically connected to muscles have no business firing when the monkey is completely still, hand in lap, watching somebody else's actions. And yet they did."[18]

Mirror neurons demonstrate that humans are fundamentally connected, confirming the idea that our being-becoming is inaugurated by another. Such information transmitters demonstrate the fact that one person's experience can be that of another's. This accidental discovery is more profound that it may seem at first glance. Mirror neurons allow for more than simply imitation; they allow us to have the same neural reaction. It is possible to know the "mental states of others," according to Iacoboni, "and we achieve this end by way of mirror neurons."[19] Experiences can be shared. When I see someone touch a hot stove, these neurons allow me to have the same neural experience as the one being burned. (I, of course, do not experience the pain, since I'm in a different context—the communication from my hand to my brain tells me that I'm not the one getting burned.) For philosopher Alvin Goldman, mirror neurons solve the dilemma of other minds, a problem created by modern philosophy and science. He writes, "If I have access only to my own mind, which is a private entity that only I can access directly, how can I possibly understand the minds of other people."[20] Mirror neurons "commit us to others." "The interdependence between self and other that mirror neurons allow shapes the social interactions between people, where the concrete encounter between self and other becomes the shared existential meaning that connects them deeply."[21]

Mirror neurons at best tell us that human beings share a cognitive and socially interconnecting reference point. But how does this transform us? How are we interlinked or rewired over time as a result of our committed social engagements? Let me restate my claim that others do not simply influence us. In many cases, they become a part of us. Recall what I wrote earlier about the death of a loved one. The living spouse hears, often sees, and has conversations with their deceased loved one. Have they lost their mind? No. They have lost, however, not so much their other (or better) half, though this is true, but rather an essential part of their being. The mind of the one who has died still exists in a very real way in the mind of the one who remains alive. Incorporating the other person into our subjective mind through our shared experience transforms both individuals. This takes time, attending religiously to one another. The more I spend time with my wife, the more I become her and she becomes me. We are a unity of two persons. Our individual identity is forever changed. I have become someone different because of my wife. As believers, the more we commune with Christ through the ordinary means of grace, the more we conform to His image. The gracious work of sanctification requires intimate communion with the Son.

Teaching and Learning Community

In the process of uncovering the mysteries of the world, we come to understand who we are. And if the dynamic self is dependent on its relation to its environment, especially its social environment, then it would be good for us to look at the communal nature of learning. Along with basic cognitive faculties, what are the social elements that contribute to a deeply engaged learning community?[22] A goal of a liberal arts curriculum should be to foster a healthy social environment. How is this done? A strong community can be achieved by connecting students to students, students to administrators, staff, and faculty members, and to each social group to the institution's mission and goals, creating a large socially dynamic network for holistic learning.

Let us consider a few practices, what Palmer calls the "hidden curriculum," for strengthening the learning community. My intent in this last portion is not to demonstrate *exactly how* a particulate community will eventually shape an individual. Each institution, given its unique mission and learning outcomes, must do this on its own. Rather, I'd like to focus on the generally applicable ways in which a college community's social base can be strengthened for the purposes of exploring innovative formative practices.

1. *The Human before Technology.* Transcendentalist writer and social critic Henry David Thoreau once presciently warned American citizens—citizens, like many today, being transformed by the items consumed in a commercial-based market society—not to "become the tools of our own tools." Nineteenth and twentieth-century social critics of industrialization referred to this as "self-alienation," whereby, as I mentioned earlier in this work, the things that we make come to enslave us, creating an altered reality where the creators serve the dictates of their creation. In regard to teaching, it is very easy to rely too much on or even hide behind technology.

A similar kind of alienation has occurred in the information age. When I began teaching college, I used technology every single day for the entire class time—PowerPoint presentations, video clips, sound bites, and so on. I came to realize that I was relying too much on these hyper-sensorial forms of communication and not on the human element necessary for teaching. The technology that I relied so heavily on disengaged human interaction. The danger of these tools is that students often tune out. So, I began to disentangle myself from such dependency, using technology only when absolutely necessary. When I use it, I make sure I'm engaging students with important questions related to a video or music bite or a painting projected on the screen. But *I* am the one teaching the class, not technology. Face-to-face interaction between instructor and student and between students strengthens the bonds of community.

2. *Demonstrate the Joy of Teaching.* Recall the importance of learning from authority as an aspect of developing biblical wisdom. Think also about how humans, consciously and subconsciously, adopt the habits of the other. As that which is inherently social, wisdom is cultivated by mimicking the wiser adult. Successful learning comes from watching an instruc-

tor's passion. As Roche says, "Modeling, even unconscious modeling, can be a much more powerful source of education than explicit discourse."[23] Most of us have had at least one teacher who has expressed great enthusiasm for the particular subject they teach. I know I have. Have you ever reflected on the educational impact of such ebullience? The positivity of the instructor contributes to a positive environment for the learner; a teacher's enthusiasm is magically infectious. The learner is more open to the content of the subject. "Professor S really loves economics," students may notice, leading them to think that perhaps that they too should love economics. When the student talks about economics, they often take on the manners of their professor. Through their bodily actions, they become convinced of the importance of the subject. It is in the enthusiasm of the teacher that makes the learning process exciting. Professors, writes Arthur Holmes, "infect their students with a love for learning and involve them in disciplined work."[24] This is part of a student's growth in maturity as Mark Bauerlein suggests: "Maturity comes, in part, through vertical modeling, relations with older people such as teachers, employers, ministers, aunts and uncles, and older siblings, along with parents, who impart adult outlooks and interests."[25] On this note, Roche cites James Freedman: "By the power of their example, professors, engaged in liberal education convey the humane significance of such values as inquiry, integrity, empathy, self-discipline, and craftsmanship."[26] The inspiring teacher has an almost magical way of passing on that inspiration to his or her students. Educators have access to a wide variety of teaching methods, but such methods (i.e., pathways) fall flat without the inspiration and excitement strategically demonstrated by an instructor. Teaching is truly a daily performance.

3. *Model the Process of Learning.* One of my goals as an educator is to get students to a place where they can engage a complex issue with little or no hand-holding, a student who reaches a level of maturity to grapple with a challenging social or cognitive issue.[27] But too often educators—top-down administers, really—demand *maturity* of students without *maturing* them. Professors need patience, an important part of wisdom, to guide their students to higher levels of engagement. When communicating a concept, instructors want students to follow a particular train of thought—reinforced through partial-learning, problem-solving practices. Instructors should guide students through the entire content, especially when it comes to teaching a particular subject. In my lower-division survey courses, I try to model what it is that a historian does. This entails making an explicit argument either every day or for every unit of study. (I understand that this may be a bit formulaic. I'm also keenly aware that history is a lot messier than when I package it in a neat argument. Even complex arguments can seem a bit too simplistic. But this seems unavoidable, for history is a cognitive activity that requires arguments.) I begin each unit or period with a clearly stated thesis—a clearly stated thesis, my students will attest to, does not exclude complexity—and then offer, at the minimum, three claims to support the thesis. Such claims come from sources I incorporate in class (primary and secondary sources that include a variety of media: literature, film, art, music, etc.). Some students (though I haven't heard any complaints yet) may become somewhat bored with the monotony of my announcement, "Here's my thesis for today, and here are my summary points," but I do this so that they too will learn how to make an argument on their own.

Upper-division classes, on the other hand, should build on the practices of the lower-level ones. Having shown students how to make an argument at the lower-level, I encourage advanced students to analyze the arguments in their earlier classes, comparing them with competing arguments, in order for them to develop—or struggling to establish—their own positions. My lower-division courses are more *constructive*, while my upper-division courses are more *deconstructive* problem-solving. The latter courses are exploratory and experimental. I want students to think at a deeper level, to take ownership of their education. This is not some sick desire of mine to exacerbate students—though I'm sure some students see the madness of my pedagogical methods in precisely this way. Rather, I wish for them to learn how to deal wisely with the ironies that more accurately characterizes reality and our perception of it.

This modeling approach requires not only clarity in making an argument, but also articulating the learning objectives for the class. An effective course is one that lays out learning objects. Students must hear from instructors what exactly they will get out of the class. Student Learning Outcomes (SLOs) are measurable tasks for students to target in a course. SLOs for a history class, for instance, look something like this: Objective #1: Students will be able to identify key dates, individuals, and periods in history; Objective #2: Students will articulate in oral and written format historiographical arguments pertaining to major historical events. SLOs for a literature class will include articulating major literary methods, schools, and authors. Those for a Bible class will include demonstrating the ability to identify authors, historical context, and articulating basic hermeneutical methods. The SLOs should be stated in the syllabus and articulated by the instructor at the beginning of the class. As it relates to community, SLOs are better accomplished with close interaction between instructor and student.

4. *Focus on Students.* Effective teachers demonstrate that they know and understand their subjects "extremely well"; consider their subject as "intellectually demanding"; expect more from their students; provide an environment that encourages students to engage big questions in critical and creative ways; and regularly self-evaluate their own methods. Added to this list is the need to demonstrate care and concern for the development of students. A student's success in the classroom depends in part on their own self-perception, which can be enhanced positively by an instructor's attitude toward them.[28] Treating students in a disrespectful, condescending, or unequal manner from other students has an adverse effect on learning and threatens student retention and, thus in both cases, the learning community as a whole.

The professor who cares for his or her students should not diminish the rigor demanded for successful learning. The difference is that successful teachers know how to push students without pushing them over the edge, so to speak. The best instructors, according to Ken Bain, author of *What the Best Teachers Do,* "look for and appreciate the individual value of each student"; they have "greater faith in students' ability to achieve"; and finally, they "set high standards," trusting in their students' "abilities to meet them."[29] They challenge, yet guide at the same time. Students should feel some stress when the instructor walks into the room; this fuels their desire to do well. Effective instructors raise students to a higher level of rigor in a course. Added to the effectiveness of a course is regular testing and prompt feedback.

5. *Be Flexible in Teaching Styles.* It's true that students respond in different ways to how material is presented in class,
making it important, therefore, for instructors to consider
employing various methods of teaching. Active learning is
all the rage today. The traditional lecture is frowned upon. It
seems to be cast as a small but enduring artifact of intellectual
imperialism. If, for some reason, students in a classroom are
not participating in some kind of cross-fit pedagogy, gyrat-
ing to burn hundreds of calories, or feeding their penchant
for immediate change, then that time of instruction, as our
educational culture would have it, has been woefully wasted.

But I'd like to question this anti-lecture culture. Any
method of teaching from lectures to "case studies, prob-
lem-based learning, powerful assignments, playing guide-by-
the-side, conducting discussions, or creating stimulating field
work" can "fail miserably," writes Bain.[30] Various exercises
that characterize active learning (which for some strange
reasons does not include the activity of sitting at a table and
taking notes while listening to an instructor) can become as
monotonous or "boring" as a lecture. People can sit through
a two-hour comedy routine, many of which are quite insightful if not directly educational, but they can't sit through an
hour-and-a-half lecture on a social, political, economic, or
cultural "hot topic"? In one sense, it seems to me, the hostili-
ty to lectures, without qualifying what a lecture entails, feeds
our culture of distraction, a culture that runs counter to the
holistic and meaningful experience that a liberal arts education strives to achieve. Instructors can lose sight of the fact
that doing different things in class can be as harmful when
it comes to educational effectiveness, especially when there
is little or no coherence tying the activities into a coherent
whole. Please do not misunderstand. I'm not at all hostile to

a variety of methods, and have, over the years, employed different strategies, but I've also incorporated new and old forms of lecturing with significant success. Pedagogy, in my mind, should never be a closed system.

6. *Employ Habits for Retention.* An important challenge faced by those who value the liberal arts is convincing others, both parents and students, of such an education's importance. Most parents and students are concerned about majors—especially so-called STEM majors (sciences, technology, engineering, and math)—that will, they assume, result in a high paying job. The importance of human fulfillment and cultivating an ethic that deepens one's love for God and neighbor is a mere afterthought—if it happens to come as a thought at all—of education today.

College professors and administrators may not have the time, resources, or energy to generate a paradigm shift when it comes to convincing people of the importance of education, but they can work to retain students and, thus, strengthen the learning community. Student retention centers on "creating a sense of belonging in students," according to Lieberman. Doing so improves "learning and educational outcomes."[31] Let me highlight the studies that have more of a direct impact on the small liberal arts college. First, retention is strengthened by a clear representation of leadership on campus. The leadership refers to cabinet-level leaders: presidents, provosts, Chief Financial Officers, Deans, Vice President for Academic Affairs, etc. Retention is threatened when key administrative officers are absent.[32] Students want to be assured that their education is backed by strong leadership. This offers to them a sense of security—security in knowing that their school and their education is firmly grounded. Let me be clear. I'm speaking simply of presence. I don't mean authoritarian leadership.

"Frequent student-faculty contact in and out of classes," according to a study done in the late 1980s, "is *the most important factor in student motivation and involvement*."[33] This relates directly to a second factor in strong retention: faculty interaction with students outside the classroom setting—having lunch in the cafeteria, inviting students over for a meal, game night, midnight exam breakfast, or, as my wife and I like to do occasionally, a film. From the student's perspective, a faculty or staff member who interacts with students outside the classroom communicates a very strong message: "Wow, this professor is really interested in *me*, not just as a student (or student number) but a human being."

Third, residence life staff members play a vital role not only in persistency and retention rates but also the health and longevity of an institution. This is a very important point. Res-life professionals handle some of the most difficult life issues. The authors of the recently published *Rethinking College Student Retention* encourage residence-life directors (R.A.s, R.D.s, Deans of Students) to create a healthy residential community of coordinated interaction that produces not only a safe and healthy environment but also an intellectually strong social community. A prospective or newly enrolled student who simply perceives the potential for a healthy community is in a better position to become socially integrated; social integration, in consequence, "positively affects subsequent institutional commitment."[34] Resident life programs, reflecting the spatial and demographic makeup of the student body, should "encourage students to socialize with other students on the floor"; participate in "hall government"; work together to maintain "hall concerns (e.g., establishing and maintaining quiet hours for studying)"; team building activities; weekly activities, including fundraising activities for a common goal;

provide access to professional help for stress and psychological needs; provide adequate training in safety and sensitivity (e.g., racial and gender) for all students and staff; and maintain efficient plans to address negative social experiences.[35]

The final two retention issues relate to student perception and so-called "buy in." Arthur Holmes writes, "When a community organizes its life to preserve or enhance or transmit those values or to undertake its task more effectively, institutions arise."[36] Prospective as well as currently enrolled students who buy into the mission of an institution or, for a Christian school, are part of the tradition to which the school aligns itself are most likely to matriculate and remain at the institution.[37] Visit days put on by admissions departments play a vital role in convincing parents and prospective students of a college's mission. And, of course, once students arrive college personnel must find ways to help incoming students transition to college life. Early orientation programs by student life, usually the first week or weeks of the first semester, peer-mentors in the first semester, "the strongest single source of influence on cognitive and affective development," and foundational courses (e.g., Christian mind and calling, great books, or special topics)—small courses considered as part of a student's first year experience (FYE)—are critical for initial success in college.[38]

Higher retention rates are attained when students perceive that they play a part in decision making at the college. The key term here is "perception." It's not that students have to be involved in every decision. Rather, they need to see that faculty and staff value their input in the direction of the college. Having a bimonthly "State of the College" address by the president or electing student representatives to sit in on staff and board meetings communicates to students that their opinions matter. Keeping vital information (e.g., financial stability) from key players—especially tuition payers—is highly precarious for an institution. A lack of transparency hurts everyone. Likewise, students want to perceive that administrators, student life personnel, and faculty members (at all levels) demonstrate their own commitment to the mission and goal of the college.[39] The vision or mission of the college, I believe, requires frequent supportive explication by faculty, staff, and board members. Every employee should memorize the mission statement of their institution and be able to articulate that mission to current and prospective students and their parents. And keeping in line with the clear presence of leadership on campus as well as a demonstration by faculty and staff of their commitment to the institution, faculty and staff should frequently attend to the practices that make up the school's dynamic ethos.

Finally, strong retention comes when students perceive that they are treated in an equal manner.[40] When students see that other students or groups of students are given preferred treatment, they feel disconnected, and their commitment to the institution begins to diminish. Professors and administrators must strive to treat students equally; they should explicate the requirements they have for students and apply them equitably. Favoritism hurts the vitality of a school, for a student will not invest in an institution if they perceive that their professors refuse to invest in them. This equally applies to student affairs: "If students feel well informed about rules and requirements pertinent to student life, then they perceive that their institution places a high value on students. If students feel that rules and regulations pertinent to them are fairly administered, then they come to perceive that their institution treats students in an equitable way."[41]

Each of the above suggestions (not exhaustive by any means) for creating and maintaining a healthy environment is applicable to all schools. But a Christian school has an additional task related to community: maintaining its Christian identity. Retention is aided by students, staff, and faculty who buy in to a school's faith tradition. But so often we see schools move away from their historical roots. How does a religious institution keep its faith tradition in light of constant social, cultural, and political pressures? In *Quality of Soul*, author Robert Benne shares his conclusions as to how six leading religious institutions have maintained their faith commitments over the years. First and foremost, Benne believes, "it is the strength of the religious tradition that makes possible its translation into a robust religious identity and mission for the school. Without a strong religious tradition—usually a church—behind it, a college can have great difficulty maintaining its religious identity and mission."[42] (A school's relationship to a church does not mean it must ultimately be operated by a particular denomination, but it certainly needs ties to a theological and ecclesiastical tradition. It would also be healthy for the institution to create some form of accountability relationship with supporting churches and denominations in the same or similar faith tradition. The historical and theological tradition is the anchor.) Benne unpacks his claim by focusing on the "vision" and "ethos" of the colleges and universities in his study.

In regard to vision, Benne makes "two interlocking claims": (1) "a thriving Christian college has a strong connection with the religious heritage of its sponsoring church or tradition" and (2) "the Christian account given by the religious tradition should constitute the organizing principle for the identity and mission of the college."[43] By "ethos" Benne refers to the various "non-curricular practices, traditions, patterns of life, and values that add as much religious character to each school as the intellectual dimension of its religious life."[44] These wider practices should likewise conform to the confessional tradition embedded in the vision of the institution.

Notes

[1]Victor Ferral, *Liberal Arts at the Brink* (Cambridge: Harvard University Press, 2011), 14.

[2]Parker Palmer, *To Know as We are Known: Education as a Spiritual Journey* (New York: HarperCollins, 1993), 20.

[3]Arthur Holmes, *The Idea of a Christian College* (Grand Rapids: Eerdmans, 1975), 85.

[4]Michael Horton highlights that Christ's descent into hell meant not only His facing the wrath of God but also "God's rejection." Michael Horton, *We Believe* (Nashville: Word, 1998), 100.

[5]Curt Thompson, *Anatomy of the Soul: Surprising Connections Between Neuroscience and Spiritual Practice That Can Transform Your Life and Relationships* (Carol Stream: Tyndale Momentum, 2010), 30.

[6]A few readers may be intrepid by the term *adaptation*. I'm using it not in a macro-evolutionary or even a teleological sense, but that our identity undergoes changes, but changes that don't take away from our unique personality. Our experiences come in degrees. Some are exciting, some are traumatic. Such experiences have a defining impact on our lives. Yet there is a radical adaptation and teleology that I presuppose—namely, the transforming work of Christ and, as a result, our new attitude and goal to love and enjoy Him forever.

[7]http://www.usatoday.com/story/news/nation/2013/06/11/real-classrooms-better-than-virtual/2412401/.

[8]http://oermap.org/evidence/low-mooc-persistence-rate-university-of-pennsylvania-coursera/.

[9]An excellent documentary discussing this topic is *Ivory Tower*.

[10]Bruce Hood, *The Illusion of Self: How the Brain Creates Identity* (New York and Oxford: Oxford University Press, 2013), 28-29. Martin Nowak, "Five Rules for the Evolution of Cooperation" *Science* 8 (December 2006): 1560-1563.

[11]Michael Gazzaniga, *The Ethical Brain: The Science of Our Moral Dilemmas* (New York: Harper Perennial, 2005), 48.

[12]Justin Barrett, *Cognitive Science, Religion, and Theology: From Human Minds to Divine Minds* (West Conshohocken: Templeton Press, 2011), 26.

[13]Richard Restak, *Naked Brain* (New York: Three Rivers Press, 2006), 105.

[14]Ibid., 59.

[15]Hood, *Illusion*,197.

[16]Ibid., 185.

[17]Marco Iacoboni, *Mirroring People: The Science of Empathy and How We Connect with Others* (New York: Picador/Farrar, Strauss, and Giroux, 2009), 9.

[18]Ibid., 11.

[19]Ibid., 34.

[20]Ibid., 263.

[21]Ibid., 265. Italics mine.

[22]The following features of effective learning are primarily for educators.

[23]Mark William Roche, *Why Choose the Liberal Arts?* (Indiana: University of Notre Dame, 2010), 169.

[24]Holmes, *Idea,* 82.

[25]Mark Bauerlein, *The Dumbest Generation: How the Digital Age Stupefies Young Americans and Jeopardizes Our Future* (New York: Tarcher/Penguin, 2009), 136.

[26]Roche, *Why Liberal Arts,* 169.

[27]This is the distinction between "fully-guided" and "partially-guided" learning. A study done by Richard E. Clark, Paul A. Kirschner, and John Sweller and published in *American Educator* in 2012 argued that fully-guided, explicit "worked-example" models of education for novices was much more effective than minimal-guided (problem solving, discovery learning, experiential learning, constructivist learning)

instruction. See Clark, Kirschner, and Sweller, "Putting Students on the Path to Learning: The Case for Fully Guided Instruction," *American Education* (Spring 2012): 6-11.

[28]Ken Bain, *What the Best College Teachers Do* (Cambridge: Harvard University Press, 2004), 139.

[29]Ibid., 73.

[30]Ibid., 99.

[31]*Social*, 277.

[32]Please note that the absence of a key administrator may not necessarily lead to the collapse of an institution. Often institutions have to go through transitions, where import leadership positions are empty for a time. As there are a number of factors contributing to retention rates, so there are a number of factors that contribute to the longevity of an institution.

[33]Arthur W. Chickering and Zelda F. Gamson, "Seven Principles for Good Practices in Undergraduate Education," *AAHE Bulletin,* 39 no. 7 (1987), 3-7.

[34]John Baxton, et. al., *Rethinking College Student Retention* (San Francisco: Jossey-Bass, 2014), 83.

[35]Ibid., 53-54.

[36]Holmes, *Idea*, 79.

[37]John Baxton, et. al., *Rethinking College Student Retention* (San Francisco: Jossey-Bass, 2014), 48.

[38]Austin, "Involvement" quote in Roche 47.

[39]Baxton, et. al. *College Retention,* 75-76.

[40]Ibid., 86.

[41]Ibid., 103. Some educators assume that retention is, first and foremost, connected to the rigors of a particular class. It may be understandable to reduce the level of rigor of a class in order to preserve retention. High standards do not necessarily hurt retention. Granted,

an instructor who unduly burdens students for whatever reason is not interested in guiding them through a rigorous course can be a detriment to retention. Of course, such authoritarianism does not qualify as teaching and, thus, the connection between instruction and retention is severed. In fact, high educational standards can strengthen retention, especially when an instructor comes alongside students in their learning journey.

[42] Robert Benne, *Quality with Soul: How Six Premier Colleges and Universities Keep Faith with Their Religious Traditions* (Grand Rapids: Eerdmans, 2001), 67.

[43] Ibid., 96.

[44] Ibid., 145.

CHAPTER 6

LEARNING AS A
SPIRITUAL EXPERIENCE

University of Michigan Professor Ed Sarath has identified a link between jazz and the "meditation and related spiritual pursuits" of mysticism.[1] "Jazz musicians provide vivid testimonies of [peak experience and transcendence] among whose characteristics are enhanced flow of ideas, mind-body coordination, communion with surroundings, and heightened well-being."[2] This inspired Sarath to create a BFA in Jazz and Contemplative Studies. Reaching the point of mastery in music (or in any creative occupation) illustrates the spiritual feel that accompanies deep learning. The music, after hours of instruction and (more hours of) practice, becomes part of the musician's identity. Master musicians can perform something that is so ingrained in their person that it seems as if they can perform without even thinking about it. It is as if they become the music they play. They can close their eyes, play through a performance, and the in process attain a transcendent and transformative moment not just for themselves but also for their audience.

To know something is to reach a state in which the distinctions between isolated bits of data and the integration of that data are seemingly erased, producing a sensation akin to a spiritual experience.

Such a high experience is not only "the culmination of human cognitive development," it is the crux of "mystical awareness."[3] A renewed interest in mysticism may move us away from the (bad) habit of atomizing reality and toward a renewed interest in how everything fits together. This chapter identifies key elements of modern mysticism—viz., part-to-whole transcendence, worshipping habits, transformative epiphanic moments (i.e., conversions)—that line up with the development of the human mind, especially as it relates to education.

Mystical Learning

Evangelicals are not all that eager to give mysticism a fair hearing, given the assumption that mystics refuse to articulate the infinite using finite language. Many have adopted the opinion of theologian Benjamin B. Warfield in his description of the mystic: "When he sinks within himself he finds feelings, not conceptions; his is an emotional, not conceptual, religion; and feelings, emotions, though not inaudible, are not articulated. As a mystic, he has no conceptual language in which to express what he feels."[4] Admittedly, there are aspects of mysticism that conflict with a confessional faith, including the idea that communion with the absolute is a total emptying of the self and that the experience of union with God ultimately cannot be communicated. But not all mystics are the same.

The contemporary mind may exhibit more of an openness to mysticism given the intellectual consequences brought about by an interconnected globe. Historical developments in the last half century have shattered an unwavering faith in the authority of the scientific method and Enlightenment reason. Today's global community has encouraged a reconceptualization of the world as integral and holistic. In *The Geography of Thought: How Asians and Westerners Think Differently and Why,* Richard Nisbett argues that people in the East have traditionally interpreted the world "in a holistic collectivist manner, noticing connections and patterns between everything."[5] The West, on the other hand, is more fragmented, centralizing the particular and fracturing the whole. But now the habits of the developed interconnected world have conditioned the mind to think in ways that are too narrow. The contemporary mind has lost sight of the obsession of the ancients to find *the* one thing that unifies all of life, whether it be *ma'at, tao,* or the all-encompassing *logos.* Noted intellectual and popular mystic Ken Wilber is optimistic about the current world. "Knowledge itself is now global. This means that, also for the first time, the sum total of human knowledge is available to us—the knowledge, experience, wisdom, and reflection of all major human civilizations—premodern, modern, and postmodern—are open to study by anyone."[6] The intellectual temperament of the global world has led to a renewed interest in mysticism.

Evelyn Underhill defines mysticism as "the art of Union with reality...The mystic is a person who has attained that union in a greater degree; or who aims at and believes in such attainment."[7] Philosophers Robert Solomon and Kathleen Higgins understand mysticism as "the transformation of consciousness to gain access to higher orders of reality than those ordinarily experienced."[8] The feeling of being united with a higher reality can only come when sincerely engaged in an area of study. And the driving motive behind this "mystical awareness" is the heart, which Underhill defines as "the in-most sanctuary of personal being, the deep root of its love and will, the very source of its life."[9]

Up to this point, I've presented *religion* in a particu-lar way—namely, as a fundamental attitude of the heart, a pre-theoretical faith commitment, and a relationship with *anything* humans may consider divine. Furthermore, I've noted that the religious heart is shaped by faithfully attending to what is considered its highest love. The word *religion* liter-ally means to read or go over again and again. As an activity, a religion grows as individuals and communities regularly recite beliefs and perform familiar habits—what we refer to as worship—to draw closer to their divinity. Worship cen-ters on repeated practices, which, over time, leads not only to a more intimate relationship with the object of worship but also to higher states of consciousness. Philosopher James K.A. Smith defines worship as "the ordering and reordering of our material being to the end for which it was meant."[10] Through liturgical activity we come to understand better the world, ourselves, and God. These higher-level insights into the nature of being are also what Newberg and d'Aquili call "unitary states."[11] As a husband and wife incorporate each other into their individual being through consistent atten-dance over time, literally growing into one another, so we too grow into the being that we consider divine. Worshiping through the means of grace intensifies our union with God and fellow believers.

This idea of worship and all that it entails can be applied to the activity of learning. "Rhythm and repetition," New-berg and d'Aquili have argued, "are elements in almost all human rituals" and "almost always involve the highest levels of thought and feeling."[12] Many thinkers today challenge the traditional idea of education as simply a matter of depositing knowledge—knowledge that is already packaged—into the mind of the learner. Author John Horgan, however, suggests that knowledge is "best understood not as discoveries plucked whole from some Platonic ether but as embodiments of the aspirations and anxieties of living, breathing individuals."[13] The idea of worship advanced by Smith is one of "a constellation of practices, rituals, and routines that inculcate a particular vision of the good life by inscribing or infusing that vision into the heart (the gut) by means of material, embodied practices."[14] Knowing, according to Meek, "is an orientation that shapes our lives, that comes to expression in our action. And it is a struggle to integrate from every corner of our experience to a coherent pattern."[15] Underscore the idea that the process of coming to know demands "our action," our "struggle to integrate." Humans gravitate toward pictures and patterns in reality. But these pictures and patterns are constructed by our active engagement as an unfolding of creation. A successful teacher is one who is able to get what students see as isolated raw data (e.g., names, dates, numbers, words, etc.) into meaningful configurations. These arrangements are deepened in the mind through ritual habit and in consultation with a guiding community and in line with a given tradition. Knowledge comes through this type of practice.

This all sounds a lot like the habits a mystic would employ to reach a unitary state. The idea that higher levels of consciousness require focal engagement of the world, a deepening of knowledge through sustained learning habits, runs counter to a traditional understanding of mysticism— namely, the idea that one needs to empty the mind and remain indefinitely in the ineffable. It is true that many mystics avoid dogma, since for while God "may be the ultimate source of all that exists…nothing can be said about God as such."[16] But how else would we know truth, goodness, beauty, or God without faithfully attending to the discussions on such things? "We know a thing only by uniting with it," says Underhill, "by assimilating it; by an interpenetration of it and ourselves. It gives itself to us, just in so far as we give ourselves to it; and it is because our outflow towards things is usually so perfunctory and so languid [so immediate and ephemeral], that our comprehension of things is so perfunctory and languid too." She continues, "Ignorance [is] the inevitable portion of those who 'keep themselves to themselves,' and stand apart, judging, analyzing the things which they have not truly known." Ken Wilber believes that achieving a mystical state requires long hours of cognitive/emotional activity. Mysticism, he says, is "like lifting weights and exercising muscles. The more you do it, the bigger the muscle gets."[17] And for David Bentley Hart, mystical attainment "begins in one's ordinary experiences of the world. What provokes us to seek the highest truth…is the immediacy with which the transcendent shows itself within the immanent."[18]

The methods of attaining an integrated state of being through sustained meditation can be very useful in higher education. Reflecting on Wilber's comments about mysticism, journalist John Horgan suggests that "if you want to learn about physics and cosmology, you must study these subjects."[19] A student can study the content of physics and cosmology in the abstract but it does not necessarily make him or her a good physicist or cosmologist. Being good at something requires compliance with instruction as well as meditation on content and methods. We get there through focused practice—lots of it. Eventually we reach a state where we can look through the parts of a discipline to see the whole and move from the whole back to the parts.

The problem with restricting an experience of this kind to intuition, sentimentality, or the ineffable is that we tend to ignore the parts of the overall experience. At some point, we need to define the object of our study. We cannot know in a more developed way the Triune God without knowing who He is. Doctrine, formulated within a historical community (Chapter 4), is crucial in this regard. I'm often perplexed—annoyed may be a better way of putting it—by those who disparage the pursuit of theological study, since, as many a pseudo-pietist assumes, it tends to conflict with a real love—and therefore a real knowledge—of God. "Doctrine is commendable, but it's no substitute for loving Jesus," I've heard many an evangelical pastor say. I must admit: I'm not always sure how to address such incoherence.

Theology is not the enemy of a deep love for God. "But studying theology," one might say, "is no guarantee that that the individual will love God more. In fact, some have fallen away." Is that the fault of theology? Once again, we need to return to the heart. It's the heart of the one studying that leads to one of two directions—a love or hatred for God. And we must keep in mind that the heart is changed by the God-word, embodied theology, Jesus Christ. When considering the question, "Who do people say that I am?" it would be inexcusable to respond, "It doesn't matter what people say, I just love You." An evangelical would never get away with saying that the content of mathematics is great, but it's no substitute for loving mathematics? Christians must focus on the *real* person and work of the Triune God. "Biblical meditation," writes Timothy Jennings, "focuses on some substantive aspect of God and His character of love."[20] They are to reflect upon God's law, words, decrees, wonders, and love (Ps. 1, 48, and 119): "God calls us to meditate *on his law of love,* which is an expression of His character of love. This is no empty, mindless, thoughtless meditation, but a contemplative, deeply reflective meditation on the beauty of our infinite God and His methods of love. Such meditation requires the balanced engagement of both right and left hemispheres. Such balance not only results in greater health and peace but also growth in Christlikeness."[21]

With our whole being we meditate on—and hence commune with—God, His love, His decrees, wonders, and laws. This is the core of Christian education. The Hebrew word for "meditate" (*haghah*) "can refer to silent musing or pondering…But its basic idea seems to involve some kind of utterance such as muttering or whispering, like talking to oneself."[22] Also the word *meditation* (*siakh*) means to rehearse "something in one's mind, either outwardly talking or musing silently."[23] The apostle Paul encouraged the members of Christ's body to "dwell on" things that are true, honorable, right, (Phil 4:8) and to set their minds on "things above" (Col. 3:2)—"to ponder, to let one's mind dwell on, to keep thinking about, to fix one's attention."[24]

Transcendence and Transformation

"If you have ever 'lost yourself' in a beautiful piece of music," Newberg and Aquili illustrate, "or felt 'swept away' by a rousing patriotic speech, you have tasted in a small but revealing way the essence of mystical union."[25] Imagine applying Sarath's methods to other disciplines in order for students to reach transformative states. We are "moved," "enlightened," or "elevated" when finally figuring something out after painstaking attendance. The willing learner seeks to creatively put together—to play with, through jazzy meditative improvisation—the parts of reality in various structured representations, moving deeper and deeper through levels of cognition that transform being, which consequently leads not only to a feeling of transcendence but also a reorientation of self in the world. For George Willis, "those people who have most intensely perceived Reality [sic]," sought an integrated union with God through His word, "may be the most ready and able to change the world for the better."[26]

As mentioned earlier, contemporary mystics have described their experience "as the absorption of the self into something larger."[27] When we progress deeper and deeper into knowing something we feel an intense intimacy with the object of knowledge like the intercourse between a husband and wife in the marriage bed. Classical thinkers called this unification of knowledge *noesis*. When knowledge matures through meditation, the knower gains a sense of interconnectedness, which, in turn, begins to blur the line between the self and the world. This stage is called *nous*, Pure Knowledge, "where the knower, known, and the knowing become One."[28] Note the two stages of knowing/being. We bring together the parts of reality on a cognitive level, which, at some point, triggers an ontological union with the whole. Willis writes, "Anyone who sincerely aspires to unite with Reality is a mystic, even before that union may be attained."[29] A moment of insight is, like mysticism, "a clear and vivid consciousness of *no-thing*. Yet it is also a sudden, vivid consciousness of *everything* as an undifferentiated whole."[30]

Focusing on the world for coherence generates the sense of going beyond the self. Stimulation of the brain's limbic system, the center of our deepest thoughts, can produce "out-of-body sensations, déjà vu, and illusions, all of which have been reported during spiritual states."[31] This is why Newberg and Aquili consider this portion of the brain as the "trans-

mitter to God." Habits that help to congeal what we love via
the limbic system allow us to gain a sense of transcendence.
"The transcendence of the self, and the blending of the self
into a larger reality," Newberg and d'Aquili claim, "is a major
goal of ritualized behavior [which] almost always involves
the highest levels of thought and feeling."[32] In activating the
limbic system, we shape the supra-temporal heart that moves
us closer to transcendence. For Malcolm Jeeves, self-tran-
scendence is the "capacity to reach out beyond oneself and
discover or make meaning of experience through broadened
perspectives and behavior."[33] It is thus through liturgies that
we can go beyond the self (i.e., transcend) to reach higher
levels of meaning. Reaching deeper levels of meaning will
intensify the sense of transcending the boundaries of the self
in order to be more intimate with the object of our meditation. We become immediately aware of our transcendence
and immanence in the cosmos.

Taking time to engage the world with a deep affection for
what will be discovered is radically transformative. We move
from the unknown to the known and are converted in the
process. To convert means "to turn from" one thing toward
something new, however acquired. It is both act and process
that transforms or changes us from one state of being to another. The brain is plastic, and if this is true then so are humans. Paying close attention to an object of study, according
to Jeffrey Schwartz, "redraws the contours of the mind...in
so doing can rewire the circuits of the brain."[34] Michael Polanyi and Harry Prosch, in their collaborative work entitled
Meaning, associate knowing with the transformative process
of conversion:

> It seems clear that we do not become converted—whether
> to a political party, a philosophy, *or* a religion—by having
> the truth of what we come to know demonstrated to us in

a wholly logical or objective way. Rather, what happens
when we become convinced is that we see at some point
that the particular party or religion or epistemology or
worldview (or even scientific theory) in front of us holds
possibilities for the attainment of richer meanings than
the one we have been getting along with. At that moment
we *are* converted, whether we have ever willed it or not.[35]

We should highlight in the above passage not only the "attainment of richer meanings," but also whether or not we've
"willed it." The moment of conversion is often unexpected.
True, we may be open to or have the desire to be converted,
but the moment of insight—a converting moment indeed—
often comes when we least expect it.

An interesting section in Meek's *A Little Manual for
Knowing* is the central place of both "the Void" and "the Holy"
in the knowing process and in human becoming. The Void—
"the deep realization that we might not exist, that we need
something, someone, beyond ourselves"—is our "coping with
our situation," opening up ourselves to where the situation
might take us.[36] Those familiar with *Loving to Know* should
be reminded of Meek's encouragement to open ourselves up
to the "contingency of being," to invite the real. Our momen-
tary (or often not-so monetary) communion with the Void
precedes our epiphanic surprises, our "AHA!" moments—
moments of clear insight. Another important function of the
Void not articulated by Meek in *Little Manual* but intimated
in *Longing to Know* is how it helps us avoid the temptation
of being, as Arthur Schopenhauer once said, "shut-up in our
own solipsistic blockhouse." It forces us to reject a pure sub-
jectivism, the philosophically unsophisticated idea that we
can create our own reality. To cast it in a more positive light,
acceptance of the Void is, in fact, an anticipatory faith in the
real. The mind is shaped by the reality that meets our faithful

invitation and indwelling of it. In fact, there is no mind apart from external reality. This relates to the second attribute of our humanness, the Holy. The Holy, the "gracious possibility of new being," according to Meek, immediately follows the "AHA!" moment. We are transformed when we embrace reality and when reality embraces us. Think again of the musician whose physicality is changed by his communing with a musical piece as well as the musical instrument. The music saturates his blood, changes habits, and moves him to see the world in a new, more enriching way.

The individual transformed by meditative experience can transform the lives of others. A mystical experience need not remain restricted to the one having the experience; it can be transferred. The gifted learner who reaches the level of mastery can also direct the experience of another. Consider the number of musicians who, while performing, can literally close their eyes to let the music—the whole piece—guide them. Not only are they enraptured by what they are doing but they have the ability to give the audience a similar experience. What I mean here is that part of reaching a real unitary state is not just the musicians' putting together notes on a page but actively interconnecting the social landscape as well. In other words, part of the transcending nature of the mystical experience is for the artist/intellectual to give the experience to others. This is possible given our neural interconnectedness. And we may wonder about the extent of such transference—from the initial subject, to another, to the entire cosmos and back. "The mystery of music," Underhill writes, "is seldom realized by those who so easily accept its gifts. Yet of all the arts music alone shares with the great mystical literature the power of waking within us a response to the life-movement of the universe: brings us—we know not how—news of its exultant passions and its incomparable peace. Beethoven heard the voice of Reality, *and little of it escaped when he translated it for our ears.*"[37] The excitement an instructor exhibits in the process of teaching his or her subject is infectious. Since humans are empathetic animals, as discussed in an earlier chapter, a student can image the neural experience occurring in the mind of the instructor.

God's creation is the network within which humans can have a real connection. We become who we were made to be by attending to—by worshiping—the Creator, communing with Him through the things the Spirit communicates to us. This is certainly not an easy task. We need to learn the steps, read the music, and allow ourselves and others to be swept up into God's poetry.

Notes

[1] Sean Esbjorn-Hargens, Jonathan Reams, Olen Gunnlaugson, eds., *Integral Education: New Directions for Higher Learning* (Albany: State University of New York, 2010), 169.

[2] Ibid., 172.

[3] John Horgan, *Rational Mysticism: Dispatches from the Border Between Science and Spirituality* (New York: Houghton Mifflin, 2003), 66.

[4] Benjamin Warfield, *Studies in Theology* (Edinburgh: Banner of Truth, 1988), 661.

[5] Nisbett quote in Bruce Hood, *The Illusion of Self: How the Social Brain Creates Identity* (New York and Oxford: Oxford University Press, 2012), 212.

[6] Ken Wilber, *Integral Spirituality* (Boston: Integral Books, 2006), 27.

[7] Evelyn Underhill, *Mysticism: The Preeminent Study in the Nature and Development of Spiritual Consciousness* (New York: Image Books, 1990), 23.

[8] Solomon and Higgins, *A Passion for Wisdom: A Very Brief History of Philosophy* (New York and Oxford: Oxford University Press, 1997), 59.

[9] Underhill, *Mysticism*, 72.

[10] James K.A. Smith, *Desiring the Kingdom: Worship, Worldview, and Cultural Formation* (Grand Rapids: Baker Academic, 2009), 143.

[11] Andrew Newberg, Emilio D'Aquili, and Vince Rause, *Why God Won't Go Away: Brain Science and the Biology of Belief* (New York: Random House, 2001), 82.

[12] Ibid., 85-86.

[13] Horgan, *Rational Mysticism*, 9.

[14] Smith, *Desiring*, 86, 90.

[15] Esther Meek, *Longing to Know: The Philosophy of Knowledge for*

Ordinary People (Grand Rapids: Brazos Press, 2003), 74.

[16]Solomon and Higgins, *Wisdom,* 60.

[17]Wilber quote in Horgan, *Rational Mysticism,* 61.

[18]David Bentley Hart, *The Experience of God: Being, Consciousness, Bliss* (New Haven: Yale University Press, 2013), 330.

[19]Wilber quote in Horgan, *Rational Mysticism,* 61.

[20]Jennings, *The God-Shaped Brain: How Changing Your View of God Transforms Your Life* (Downers Grove: InterVarsity Press, 2013), 226.

[21]Ibid.

[22]Robert Saucy, *Minding the Heart: The Way of Spiritual Transformation* (Grand Rapids: Kregel, 2013), 153.

[23]Ibid.

[24]Ibid., 154.

[25]Eugene d'Aquili and Andrew Newberg, *The Mystical Mind: Probing the Biology of Religious Experience* (Minneapolis: Augsburg Fortress, 1999), 37.

[26]George Willis, "Spirituality, Mysticism, the Arts, and Education" *Educational Horizons* (Summer 2000), 175.

[27]Newberg, Aquili, Rause, *Why God Won't,* 6.

[28]Anthony Ashton, et. al., *Quadrivium: The Four Classical Liberal Arts of Number, Geometry, Music, and Cosmology* (New York: Bloomsbury, 2010), 4.

[29]George Willis, "Spirituality, Mysticism, the Arts, and Education," *Educational Horizons* (Summer 2000), 173.

[30]Philip F. Gura, *American Transcendentalism: A History* (New York: Hill and Wang, 2007), 147.

[31]Ibid., 42. See also Albright and Ashbrook, 72.

[32]Newberg and Aquili, *The Mystical Mind,* 80, 82, 85. See also New-

berg, Aquili, and Rause, *Why God Won't Go Away,* 85. M.W. Hopper and F.S. Vogel, "The Limbic System in Alzheimer's Disease: A Neuro-pathological Investigation" *The American Journal of Pathology* 85, no. 1 (October 1976): 1-20.

[33] Malcolm Jeeves, *Minds, Brains, Souls and God: A Conversation on Faith Psychology and Neuroscience* (Downers Grove: Intervarsity Press, 2013), 142, 144-45.

[34] Jeffrey Schwartz, *The Mind and the Brain: Neuroplasticity and the Power of Mental Force* (New York: HarperCollins, 2002), 330, 332, 339.

[35] Michael Polyani and Harry Prosch, *Meaning* (Chicago: University of Chicago, 1975), 179-80.

[36] Esther L. Meek, *Little Manual on Knowing* (Eugene: Cascade, 2014), 35.

[37] Evelyn Underhill, *Mysticism: A Study in the Nature and Develop-ment of Man's Spiritual Consciousness* (New York: Meridian Books Noonday Press, 1955), 76-77.

WHY ATTEND A REFORMED LIBERAL ARTS COLLEGE?

The goal of this book has been to offer a nuanced defense of the importance of a thoroughly biblical liberal arts education. Such an education values the sovereignty of God in all of life, recognizes the root of faith that drives knowing and being, and seeks through a diverse curriculum an understanding of the interconnectedness of life in the pursuit of meaning— all with the goal of reaching higher states of consciousness, a transformed self, and closer contact and knowledge of the Creator.

Yet the question remains: Why attend a Christian liberal arts institution?

A liberal arts curriculum reflects an understanding of the interdependence of various disciplines and how they work together to provide a richly meaningful educational experience. A more diverse education will yield numerous patterns—patterns that reveal the harmony, balance, and proportion of the world. It will yield a picture of the world that reflects God's own being—a unity in plurality. Every piece of knowledge

from the remedial to the advanced is true based on its pro-
portionality. The necessary conclusion "4" from the premises
"2" and "2" and the function of the "+" sign is true precisely
because it is balanced, a balance that strengthens our faith
that such a truth has remained consistent over time. And the
deeper one goes in the knowledge arena the richer the balance, harmony, and proportion.

Second, God calls us to meditate on that which is good,
true, and beautiful. If we believe that beauty and goodness are
a matter of balance and proportion, as in the Greek notion
of *kalon* (beauty or good), then the two are inextricably tied
to—if not the same as—truth. If we come to the realization
that a work of art is beautiful or an act of justice is good, then
we should feel confident to say that such a work of art or act
of justice is also true. In the latter portion of his letter to the
Ephesians, Paul encourages the church at Ephesus to walk in
love, the transformative love of Christ freely given to believers, and live distinctively pure and holy lives in order to shine
the light of Christ to the world. Christians are to walk in love
by living in the light. But what is often forgotten in this portion of Paul's letter is that the fruit of that gospel-driven light
is also found in all that is "good," "right," and "true." Thus, why
do we think on these things? We do so because they illumi-
nate the Gospel of Christ.

Finally, such an education nurtures the religious core of
being. When we encounter harmony, balance, and proportion—i.e., truth, goodness, and beauty—we feel an intimate
connection with realities beyond the self. The richer the coherence and hence the deeper the truth, goodness, and beauty
the greater connection or intimacy we feel with the world. At
the same time, it leads to a very real sense of transcendence,
a connection with something higher, something ultimate.
These are the same feelings we get when we have a religious

experience, the moments of oneness with God. Our engagement with the good, the true, and the beautiful is the door that leads to greater knowledge of God. It says in chapter 13 of the Wisdom of Solomon that an encounter with beauty brings at the same time a "corresponding perception of the Creator." This should be the most convincing reason for why a young person (or adult) should attend a Christian liberal arts institution. A liberal arts education offers a "corresponding perception" of the divine. The final moral question, then, relates to how we should respond. As I've tried to make clear, our religious ground motive will guide us toward one of two responses: submission or rebellion.

Christian institutions of higher learning provide an opportunity to contemplate the human subject in the great scope of reality, to learn to love—and live—with other people, and to learn how to know God more. Some may reply by saying that a person can do all that without attending college at all. This is true. An environment deprived of an explicitly Christian approach to learning may not be a detriment to an individual's faith. But what is certain is that not taking advantage of such an institution will reduce the time that could be spent growing in the faith. This is not to say that the Christian college environment quarantines young people from the world, the flesh, and the devil. Indeed, an institution does not have long to live if it is created solely to protect the innocent from the world.

The success of a Christian institution comes in how it lovingly invites reality in order to find what God has declared "good" in it. A Christian liberal arts institution encourages students to embrace the invitation of participating in the unfolding of creation in order to discover their true self and a greater knowledge of the Creator.

About Falls City Press

Falls City Press is an independent publishing house with the mission of serving authors as they deserve, so they can write the books we all should read.

Established in 2014, Falls City Press is nestled in the Beaver River Valley in Western Pennsylvania.

In all of their work, the staff of Falls City Press is committed to the flourising of readers, writers, and their local communities.

www.fallscitypress.com

Also from Falls City Press

Storied Leadership:
Living and Leading from the Christian Narrative

by Brian Jensen and Keith R. Martel

Are you looking for something more than leadership tips, tricks, and techniques?

Are you longing for a perspective on leadership that is developed from the rich story of the Scriptures?

Storied Leadership offers just that.

Jensen and Martel take their readers on a journey through the biblical narrative, drawing out rich and poignant ways that the Scriptures help us to understand the world, so that we can live and lead more authentically.

Storied Leadership offers an encounter that will help anyone—from the pastor to the stay-at-home-parent to the CEO to the college student—influence faithfully in a world groaning for redemption.

Also from Falls City Press

Unleashing Opportunity:

Why Escaping Poverty Requires a Shared Vision of Justice

by Michael Gerson, Stephanie Summers, and Katie Thompson

There is a perfect storm undermining something important about America: the opportunity for people born into poverty to advance over their lifetimes.

This book explores how to unleash opportunity in five key areas: early childhood, the graduation gap, foster care, juvenile justice, and predatory lending.

For each issue, Gerson explores the magnitude of the problem, Summers applies a theological framework for considering solutions, and Thompson tells the story of men and women who have journeyed through these issues.

Social mobility has become increasingly stalled in America and the result is a class system in which birth equals destiny. *Unleashing Opportunity* is now more important than ever.

Made in the USA
Coppell, TX
04 August 2021

59916932R00100